Between the Lines

Jean Hayhoe

Richard Taylor

Mike Hayhoe

HEINEMANN
EDUCATIONAL

Heinemann Educational
a division of
Heinemann Educational Books Ltd
Halley Court, Jordan Hill, Oxford OX2 8EJ
OXFORD LONDON EDINBURGH
MADRID ATHENS BOLOGNA PARIS
MELBOURNE SYDNEY AUCKLAND SINGAPORE TOKYO
IBADAN NAIROBI HARARE GABORONE
PORTSMOUTH NH (USA)

ISBN 0 435 14001 9

British Library Cataloguing in Publication Data
Hayhoe, Jean
    Between the lines: a poetry course for GCSE.–(English
    in action).
    1. Poetry. Appreciation
    I. Title II. Taylor, Richard III. Hayhoe, Mike IV.
    Series
    809.1'001

First published in 1990
Reprinted 1991
Copyright © Jean Hayhoe,
Mike Hayhoe, Richard Taylor

Cover design by Design Revolution
Cover illustrations by Paul Collicutt

Design & typesetting by DP Press, Sevenoaks, Kent

Illustrations by David Farris, Juliette Nicholson, Clyde
Pearson, John Plumb, Robin Warburton and Oliver Wilson

Printed and bound in Great Britain by
Thomson Litho Ltd, East Kilbride, Scotland

Contents

PART TWO

Introduction

Welcome to *Between the Lines*

This is a poetry book with a difference. Like all good poetry books, it introduces you to an interesting and exciting variety of poems – but *Between the Lines* is different because it also equips you with many ways to read, explore and enjoy the poems.

Part One

Part One introduces you to a wide variety of skills to help you to read and explore poems more effectively. Each section:

- provides a poem to read and explore
- introduces the skill you are going to develop
- gives you ideas for further study and often provides suggestions for coursework.

Symbols for Coursework

Symbols appear next to each 'Suggestion for Coursework' to tell you whether the activity is suitable for **English, English Literature** or both and whether it will provide all or part of a piece of coursework. The key is as follows:

e l   – Suitable for both English and English Literature and for Dual Certification. Makes a whole piece of coursework.

e   – Suitable for English only. Makes a whole piece of coursework.

l   – Suitable for English Literature only. Makes a whole piece of coursework.

e   – Suitable for English only. Makes part of a piece of coursework.

o   – Oral work.

Most of the sections end with *Signposts*. These guide you to poems in Part Two which you can link to the poems, themes and techniques you have been studying.

Part Two

This is an anthology of poems which are listed in alphabetical order of titles. They can be enjoyed in many ways. You can:

- browse freely through the poems
- use *Signposts* from Part One to find your way to linked poems
- make your own links between poems.

The **Skills Grid** on page iv will help you to find the topics you want to practise.

We hope you enjoy the poems and the skills you develop as you use *Between the Lines.*

Best wishes,

Jean Hayhoe
Richard Taylor
Mike Hayhoe

skills Grid

Notes	In poetic forms	Story/fable	Describing	Letters/reports	Newspapers	Film and playscripting	Autobiography	Themes and anthologies	Comparison/contrast	Commenting on sound	Commenting on the visual	Commenting from notes	Shared exploration	Presenting poems and ideas	Reading aloud/taping	EXPLORATION	COURSEWORK
●			●					●				●	○	○		11, 81	6, 7, 25, 60, 66
●		●					●		○		○	●	○			13, 17, 49	
●			●						○			●	○			1, 63, 70	
●			●					●	○		○	●	○	●	○		5, 21, 49, 58, 63, 71
●	●	●						●	○		○	●	○			75, 80	15, 16, 44, 49, 58, 80
●		●		●		●		●	●	○	○	●	○			3, 36	22, 45, 61, 31, 80
●		●				●		●	●	●	●	●	○			8, 55, 62, 70, 73	
●						●			○	●	●	●	○			23, 54, 60, 66, 77	
	●	●	●					●	○		○	○	○				17, 32, 48, 53, 55, 63
●									○	●	●	●	○				13, 16, 20, 49, 55
●	●		●							●		●	○		○	57	
●	●							●	●				○		○		
●	●							●	○			●	○	○	○	16, 30, 39, 40, 54, 60	
●	●							●	●	●	○		○		○	6, 16, 24, 34	15, 16, 70
●	●									●	●	●	○				
●	●							●	●	●	●	●	○			8, 18, 54, 56, 65	2, 22, 31, 39, 40, 50, 76
●									●	○	○	○	○	○			
●	●		●						●			●	○	○	○		
●		●				●			○			●	○	○		18, 23	1, 5, 41
●	●	●				●			●			○	○	○		26, 28, 31	
●					●	●		●	○			○	○	○	○	26, 31, 76	14, 20, 43, 45, 52
●	●						●	●	○			●	○	○		4, 29, 51, 57, 59	5, 19, 22, 43, 44, 51
●									○	○		○	○	○	○		8, 10, 16, 18, 23, 32, 53, 62, 64, 68, 72
●	●	●		●			●	●				○	○	○	○	61, 70, 76, 81	17, 38, 55, 74
●		●		●								●	○	○		20, 50, 61	62, 80

ix

Part

1

Words that Open a Poem's Doors

Purpose: to see how certain words or phrases in a poem help us to 'unlock' it.

Written in the year Chi-hai (879), I

The submerged country, river and hill, is a battleground.
How can the common people enjoy their wood-cutting
  and their fuel-gathering?
I charge thee, sir not to talk of high honours;
A single general achieves fame on the rotting bones of
  ten thousand.

Ts'ao Sung

Leading in

Sometimes when you read a poem, certain words particularly strike you. They may be puzzling at first but, once you've read the poem a few times, these 'key words' may help open doors into it.

Often, titles help unlock poems, but the only title we have for this poem is: 'Written in the year Chi-hai (879), I.

Thinking about the poem

1 Read the poem again and write down four words which particularly strike you.

2 Alongside each of these 'key words', write freely about the thoughts and feelings you get from it. If any of them also puzzles you, write down the questions it raises in your mind.

3 With a partner make a list of all the key words you chose. Sharing your jottings, write down your reasons for choosing each word.

4 Read the poem on your own. Then, together, narrow your combined list down to four words which you agree are 'keys' to the poem. Make notes so that you can explain to others in the class why you have chosen each word.

5 Listen to other people's ideas. Do their key words and reasons for choosing them open further doors into the poem for you?

6 With your partner create a title which catches what you now feel the whole poem is about. Write this down, with at least three reasons for your choice.

Coursework ideas

e 1 Use your title to write an equally brief poem giving an ordinary person's feelings about war.

e 2 Write a speech by a general justifying war to ordinary people.

e l 3 Write a piece, based on your notes and what you have said and heard, in order to explore the effect that individual words in the poem have had on your thoughts and feelings. Don't feel limited to just four words.

e 4 Write a descriptive piece in prose or poetry showing in detail the effects of war on ordinary people's lives. You may use your knowledge of other literature or films to help you.

e l 5 Look at other poems about people experiencing war and write about the different ways poets deal with this theme.

Signposts Further poems which lend themselves to this approach are 11, 81.

Poems which could link with coursework assignments are 6, 7, 25, 60, 66.

Submerged – hidden, always there
Battleground – the land is to be fought over   Single general – murderer, high class high honours – battle honours, meaningless   arrogant, class issue
bones – less than human now, no respect   One man's glory...

Patterns Among Words

> **Purpose:** to see how a poet can signal mood to us by very careful and deliberate juxtapositions of words.

Leading in

It is possible to spend so long looking at bits of a poem that it dies. Nevertheless, it can be handy to run a quick eye over the vocabulary that a poem uses. For example, the poet might be expecting us to pick up certain signals from the language patterns.

What sort of atmosphere and feelings does each of the following nouns suggest to you?

Child	**Street**	**Dog**	**Home**	**Trees**
Door	**Bird**	**Song**	**Village**	**Gates**

Jot down your responses – single words or short phrases will be fine.

> By sundown we came to a hidden village
> Where all the air was still
> And no sound met our tired ears, save
> For the sorry drip of rain from blackened trees
> And the melancholy song of swinging gates.
> Then through a broken pane some of us saw
> A dead bird in a rusting cage, still
> Pressing his thin tattered breast against the bars,
> His beak wide open. And
> As we hurried through the weed-grown street,
> A gaunt dog started up from some dark place
> And shambled off on legs as thin as sticks
> Into the wood, to die at least in peace.
> No one had told us victory was like this;
> Not one amongst us would have eaten bread
> Before he'd filled the mouth of the grey child
> That sprawled, stiff as a stone, before the shattered door.
> There was not one who did not think of home.
>
> *Henry Treece*

Thinking about the poem

1 Read the poem again, a little more slowly, to understand its story.

2 What did this poem make you feel?

3 Compare these feelings with what you wrote about the list of nouns. Find those nouns in the poem and write them in the order they appear in a list.

Noun	Adjective (if any)	Comment
Village		
Trees		
Gates		

4 Now list any adjectives attached to these nouns in the **Adjective** column. With your partner, discuss how each adjective changes the atmosphere and feelings you obtained from each noun on its own. Write your brief comments in the **Comment** column.

5 Henry Treece loads almost every noun with an adjective in this poem. Read the poem again and look back over your notes. If you had to choose a title for the poem which used a noun and an adjective, what would it be? Write a paragraph showing how your title relates to the whole poem. (Henry Treece called his poem *Conquerors*.)

Coursework ideas

(e l) **1** 'There was not one who did not think of home.' Using the details and mood of the poem, write your thoughts and feelings as you go through the village. Put yourself in the place of a soldier, a refugee from another village or someone returning home to this violently altered place.

(e) **2** Write another version of this poem which uses the same setting and creatures. It could be from the viewpoint of a survivor hiding somewhere in the village, with the poem beginning with the line:

At sundown they came to our hidden village.

It could be from the viewpoint of someone returning to their home in peacetime, long before the destruction ever took place, with the opening line being:

By sundown I (or 'we') came to our hidden village.

Keep all the versions of your poem and a writing diary. Then describe to your reader the process of writing that you have been through and explain what you have tried to achieve in your poem's final version.

(e l) **3** Find at least eight 'bits' (lines, phrases or words) which have a strong effect on you. Quote them and underneath each one explain how it achieves its effect in the poem. Then sum up in a final paragraph your views of the whole poem.

Further poems which lend themselves to this approach are 13, 17, 49.

Dead or Alive?

Purpose: to explore the technique of describing the inanimate as if it is alive and vice-versa.

Landscape With One Figure

The shipyard cranes have come down again
To drink at the river, turning their long necks
And saying to their reflections on the Clyde,
"How noble we are."

The fields are waiting for them to come over.
The trees gesticulate into the rain,
The nerves of grasses quiver at their tips.
Come over and join us in the wet grass!

The wings of gulls in the distance wave
Like handkerchiefs after departing emigrants.
A tug sniffs up the river, looking like itself.
Waves fall from their small heights on river mud.

If I could sleep standing, I would wait here
Forever, become a landmark, something fixed
For tug crews or seabound passengers to point at,
An example of being a part of a place.

Douglas Dunn

Leading in

We often talk about people by referring to them in terms of things which are not living, for example: 'He's a dry old stick', 'She's a rough diamond'. We can also reverse this – we can talk about non-living things by using human or animal characteristics. We talk of a ship, or even a hurricane, as 'she'. We talk of a machine 'purring' or the wind 'howling'. Linking something which is not alive with something which is makes us more alert readers.

We call this linking of things which have some features in common *analogy*.

Thinking about the poem

1 Look again at the first verse. Create a sketch of what you see.

2 Draw two columns on a sheet of rough paper. In the left hand column, jot down each of the things which Dunn sets out to make come alive in the first three verses. In the right hand column, make brief notes on how he does so. If it helps, make further sketches as you go along. For example, your notes might say:

> *tall shipyard cranes*   *treats them like animals which have come to drink – cattle – or are they more like giraffes?*

3 Share your notes with a partner. Discuss the way that Dunn has made the things on your list seem strange and new to you.

4 Look at the last verse and what the poet wishes he might be. Sketch the scene and then discuss with your partner how this verse is different from the first three.

Coursework ideas

e 1 Think of a familiar scene or event (such as going to work in the morning). Write about it, describing *things* as if they are alive, just as the poet has done. At the end, give your reasons for your choice of analogies.

el 2 Using your notes from the lesson, write an account of Dunn's poem. Comment on what his technique of making things seem alive has done for you as you have studied the poem.

Further poems which lend themselves to this approach are 1, 63, 70.

Well, It's Like This

Purpose: to explore how a poet can economise on words by creating effects through similes.

from **Bat**

Swallows?

Dark air-life looping
Yet missing the pure loop. . .
a twitch, a twitter, an elastic shudder in flight
And serrated wings against the sky.
Like a glove, a black glove thrown up at the light,
And falling back.

D.H. Lawrence

Leading in

'You eat like a pig.'

That's hard on pigs, perhaps, but an everyday example of the way we describe one thing by likening it to something else. If you've seen and heard pigs eating, this comparison calls up pictures and sounds which are natural enough for pigs but unflattering when applied to yourself. Expressions which obviously draw your attention to a comparison by using 'like', 'as', 'as if' or 'as though' are called *similes*. Successful similes force you to use your memory and imagination when you hear or read them.

Continuing this description of a bat he saw in Italy, D.H. Lawrence wrote that it had:

'Wings like bits of umbrella'.

18

Thinking about the poem

1 Work with a partner. Begin by sketching an umbrella from different angles. Then discuss all the ways in which bits of it are like a bat's wings. You may find it easier to explain your ideas with the aid of more sketches.

2 With the help of your sketches, explain the similarities you have found to another pair. Have they noticed anything you haven't?

3 Contribute your ideas to a full class discussion. Which senses do these ideas involve? Note down any comparisons others have found that you like. Note which senses they involve.

Coursework ideas

_e l_ 1 Use your notes to explain as clearly as you can in words alone all the similarities between a bat's wings and bits of an umbrella which you now find effective.

_o_ 2 Play the Simile Guessing Game

    1 In groups, invent six similes which describe features of a thing, animal or person.

    2 Feed one simile clue at a time to the rest of the class.

    3 All of the other groups have fifteen seconds to discuss the clue. They can announce their guess by raising hands. A right guess scores for the group; a wrong guess scores against it. For example, 'It looks like an upside-down boat.' 'It moves as if it's on ice.' 'In front of it your jeans look like a rough sea; behind it, they look like a freshly laid road.'

    4 Discuss the effectiveness of the simile clues which groups invent.

_e_ 3 Write a detailed description of something no-one will ever have seen – a landscape on an imaginary planet, for example, or a fantastic animal. Aim to build in several similes, comparing the unfamiliar features to things that your reader will be able to remember and imagine.

_e l_ 4 As you read other poems over the next weeks or months, keep a record of any similes you find particularly effective and details of the poems they are in. When you have a good collection, choose your 'Top Ten' (or more) and make a written or taped anthology, with a commentary on why you like each simile.

Poems which could link with coursework assignments are 5, 21, 49, 58, 63, 71.

Seeing Things Differently

Purpose: to explore how poets can use metaphors to appeal to our five senses, our intelligence and our emotions.

Movements

Lark drives invisible pitons in the air
And hauls itself up the face of space.
Mouse stops itself being comma and clockworks on the floor.
Cats spill from walls. Swans undulate through clouds.
Eel drills through darkness its malignant face.

Fox, smouldering through the heather bushes, bursts
A bomb of grouse. A speck of air grows thick
And is a hornet. When a gannet dives
It's a white anchor falling. And when it lands
Umbrella heron becomes walking-stick.

I think these movements and become them, here,
In this room's stillness, none of them about,
And relish them all – until I think of where,
Thrashed by a crook, the cursive adder writes
Quick V's and Q's in the dust and rubs them out.

Norman MacCaig

One or two of those words might be new to you.

Piton   Spike driven into a rock to support a climber or a climbing rope
Undulate   To move in a wavy manner, up and down
Malignant   Showing intense ill will
Smouldering   Burning but without flame; on the point of bursting into flames
Relish   Get pleasure from
Cursive   Joined-up handwriting

Leading in

Even the most ordinary of language uses metaphors:

She sailed into the room and dropped anchor.

'Sailed' brings to mind someone with billowing clothes who moves almost unstoppably. 'Dropped anchor' suggests her sitting down heavily with no intention of moving for anybody. Three words of the original sentence take almost ten times as many to explain – and the explanation is nowhere near as effective. That's the economy of language that metaphors can achieve!

The minute we realise that 'sailed' and 'dropped anchor' have been transferred from their usual sea-faring setting to one we did not expect, we react with surprise, then recognition – a sort of 'Oops! . . . Of course!' That is how *metaphors* work. They challenge us to find similarities between one item and another. Unlike similes, they avoid using 'like' or 'as'. They choose to be briefer, more punchy, often more surprising.

Thinking about the poem

1 A poet often makes us use our five senses – sound, taste, touch, smell and sight. Each sense can refer to more than one physical sensation. Touch, for instance, can refer to anything sensed through the skin – texture, pressure, weight, temperature. For example, think about:

   Fox, smouldering through the heather bushes.

   This involves *sight*, the hint of redness, as slow moving as a fuse's red glowing, but it also involves *touch*, it's hot, almost ready to burst into flames.

   You can also use sense details as clues about other things – for instance, age, mood, etc. Thinking about 'smouldering' and touch, you might also have:

   The fox is hot with bloodlust, not just physically hot.

2 On your own, choose three of the metaphors in the poem which you particularly like and make notes on how they call upon your five senses. Add notes on other thoughts and feelings they stir in you.

3 Using your notes to help you, share your choice of metaphors and your insights in a group.

4 As a team, work through all the metaphors, sharing your responses to the whole poem.

Coursework ideas

el) 1 Using your notes, write about what you have found in this poem.

e 2 Using metaphors where you can, write a poem which involves energy and movement. Animals make good subjects, but what about machines, weather, various sorts of crowds?

e 3 Write a short story which begins with the same excitement and energy as this you wish.)

el) 4 Read some more poems about animals. Write about one (or more) which you think best describes an animal or animals. What seems to have interested the poet? What have you liked about the poet's way of writing?

Further poems which lend themselves to this approach are 75, 80. Poems which could link with coursework assignments are 15, 16, 44, 49, 55, 58, 80

A Flaming Nuisance

> **Purpose:** to explore how a poem can be given energy as well as form by using a family of related references.

Incendiary

That one small boy with a face like pallid cheese
And burnt-out little eyes could make a blaze
As brazen, fierce and huge, as red and gold
And zany yellow as the one that spoiled
Three thousand guineas worth of property
And crops at Godwin's Farm on Sunday
Is frightening – as fact and metaphor:
An ordinary match intended for
The lighting of a pipe or kitchen fire
Misused may set a whole menagerie
Of flame-fanged tigers roaring hungrily.
And frightening, too, that one small boy should set
The sky on fire and choke the stars to heat
Such skinny limbs and such a little heart
Which would have been content with one warm kiss
Had there been anyone to offer this.

Vernon Scannell

Leading in

Ask some people what they associate with the word 'fire', and they'll say 'Warmth, comfort, log fires' – positive things. Others will say 'Destruction, danger' – negative things. Of course, fire can provide both kinds of experience.

In everyday speech, we hear people talking figuratively about fire, heat and burning: e.g. 'a fiery temper', 'burning with passion', 'set the crowd alight'. These are metaphors. They compare one thing (for example, a person's temper) to another (a burning fire), without using the word 'like'.

Fire and fires are fascinating to many people, especially 'arsonists' – people who deliberately set fire to things.

Thinking about the poem

1 The poem is full of images of fire, burning and warmth. How many can you find?

2 Divide your page into two columns: **Literal** and **Metaphorical**. With a partner, jot down all the words or phrases which refer to fire, heat or warmth. Put them in the column you think best. Do it like this:

Literal (i.e. plain, ordinary statement)	**Metaphorical**
An ordinary match intended for. .	*burnt-out little eyes*

Compare your lists with others. Discuss any disagreements.

3 Look again at your columns and discuss the thoughts and feelings you get from the different words and phrases. The phrase 'burnt-out little eyes', suggests he is tired, worn out, eyes red like cigarette ends or perhaps blackened, like a used match. Do you agree?

4 Put a **P** against any words and phrases in your columns which seem to you to have positive, pleasant associations in the poem and an **N** against those which seem to have negative, destructive associations. Put a question mark against any you find difficult to judge.

5 What emotions does the poet invite you to feel in this poem? How do the images of fire and warmth stir up these emotions in you?

Coursework ideas

e 1 Write a story about the boy in the poem. Carefully choose a few episodes which show us in detail the circumstances of his life as well as what he did. Thinking about the last two lines may help a lot.

e 2 Write the dialogue between the boy and a policeman who interviews him about his crime at a police station.

e 3 Before he appears in court, a social worker writes a report about the boy and his home circumstances. Write this report in a style suitable to be presented to the magistrates.

e l 4 Find other poems about children under pressure and write about their circumstances and the ways in which they have been affected by the pressures in their lives. Provide evidence from the poems, quoting if possible.

e l 5 A poem which relies upon a family of images is said to use a 'motif' or 'extended metaphor'. Use your lesson notes to explore your thoughts and feelings about the individual images in 'Incendiary' and about how the 'extended metaphor' unites and gives power to the poem. Find and write about other poems which use extended metaphors.

 Further poems which lend themselves to this approach are 3, 36. Poems which could link with coursework assignments are 22, 45, 61, 71, 80

Chains of Images

Purpose: to help you explore a poem by drawing out the sequence of pictures which it enables you to make in your mind.

John Mouldy

I spied John Mouldy in his cellar,
Deep down twenty steps of stone;
In the dusk he sat a-smiling
Smiling there alone.

He read no book, he snuffed no candle;
The rats ran in, the rats ran out,
And far and near, the drip of water
Went whisp'ring about.

The dusk was still, with dew a-falling,
I saw the Dog-star bleak and grim,
I saw a slim brown rat of Norway
Creep over him.

I spied John Mouldy in his cellar,
Deep down twenty steps of stone;
In the dusk he sat a-smiling
Smiling there alone.

Walter de la Mare

Leading in

A poem, like a film, often depends on a series of pictures – 'images'. In a film, suspense can be built up by presenting the viewer with a sequence of shots which suggests a lot but deliberately does not provide a clear-cut or complete story-line. The viewer is given the chance to puzzle out what is happening or has happened.

A string of images can be used in the same way in a poem. Read the poem again to yourself and try to visualise the shots of a film version. Some of the words may also suggest sounds to you.

Thinking about the poem

1 Talk about your ideas for the shots and sound effects with a partner.

2 Make notes of your film ideas using three columns, **Picture**, **Sound** and **Motivated by.** Before you start, refer to the film scripting layout on p 29.

In column 1, describe, with a quick sketch if you like, what is in each shot. Number each shot.

Decide what sort of shot each one is. Is it a closeup, long shot, medium shot?

For column 2, decide on any sound needed – sound effects (FX), music, words.

3 Film makers talk about a shot being 'motivated'. They mean that there needs to be a reason for each shot. With a partner, look at your ideas for each shot and any accompanying sound effect. Which words or phrases in the poem have 'motivated' each?

In column 3, write these down alongside the shots and sounds they refer to.

4 You should now be in a position to say which words and phrases in the poem help you to imagine the scenes most clearly.

5 At the end, just when we expect the poem to give us a big clue as to what it is about, the last verse simply repeats the first – very mysterious. The images (sights and sounds) that you have found in the poem should help you as you consider what might have led up to the scenes described in the poem. Share your theories with others in the class.

Coursework ideas

e 1 Write a story about what might have happened to bring 'John Mouldy' to the situation shown in the poem.

e l 2 Use your Film Ideas notes to write about the effect the poem has on you. Use references and quotations to show where the poem has made you sense things physically, made you feel emotions or given you clues about John Mouldy and his circumstances.

e l 3 Find two other poems which seem to you to be deliberately mysterious. Explore how they use images of sight and sound, layout (and anything else!) to build up the mystery.

Further poems which lend themselves to this approach are 8, 55, 62, 70, 73.

Film Director

Purpose: to get to know a poem better by turning it into a film script.

First Frost

A girl is freezing in a telephone booth,
huddled in her flimsy coat,
her face stained by tears
and smeared with lipstick.

She breathes on her thin little fingers.
Fingers like ice. Glass beads in her ears.

She has to beat her way back alone
down the icy street.

First frost. A beginning of losses.
The first frost of telephone phrases.

It is the start of winter glittering on her cheek,
the first frost of having been hurt.

Andrei Voznesensky
Translated by Stanley Kunitz

Leading in

Most pop singles rely on their videos to boost sales, but there are a few singers who won't use them. They believe that people should be free to imagine their own pictures from the lyrics.

Imagining your own pictures can be a good way of getting into some poems.

Re-read this poem and picture it as you read it.

Thinking about the poem

1 On your own or with a partner, prepare your 'story board' for a filmed version of the poem. Look at p 29 to help you with types of 'shots'.

2 Beautiful drawing is not important. Use quick sketches. Start a new shot each time you want to show something different. Sometimes you will need one shot per line, but at others you may need to cut to a different shot more (or less) frequently.

3 You will probably find that you need to vary types of shot. If you are working with a partner, agree upon the shots to be used and why you want them.

4 When you've finished look at your storyboard and re-read the poem. Has your storyboard caught the poem as you wanted it to?

5 Use your sketches and the poem to help share your film ideas with someone else. You may want to include extra details you couldn't draw. Look at someone else's version and listen to what they have to say about it.

Coursework ideas

 1 **Part 1** Using 'Laying out a Film-script' (p. 29) to help you, make a complete, improved version of your film ideas for this poem. You will have to think about the kind of sound track you will need.

Do you wish to use any of the words of the poem? Where will they come in the film-script? What sort of voice? How will they be spoken?

What about sound effects?

Do you want any music? Perhaps you have certain instruments in mind or a passage of music you know.

Part 2 Include a copy of this poem and write explaining which lines, phrases or even individual words in the poem gave you most help in planning your film script. Be precise about the pictures and sounds each of these gave you.

 2 Many other poems can be approached in this way. Try this technique with another poem. Include the kinds of information asked for in Part 2 above.

 Further poems which lend themselves to this approach are 23, 54, 60, 66, 77.

Storyboard

This is a storyboard for the section of 'Goldilocks and the Three Bears'.

The idea of a storyboard is to help you visualise a story (that is, to see it in picture form, like a film or video).

Choose what you think are the most important events in the story or poem. Decide whether each frame should be a close up or a long shot (see page 29). Try to use a variety of shots in your storyboard.

Draw quick sketches.
Use an oblong frame, like a film screen or television screen.

Types of shot

BCU
Big Close Up

CU
Close Up

MS
Medium Shot

2S
2 (person) Shot

LS
Long Shot

VLS
Very Long Shot

Laying Out a Film-script

Lay your complete film-script out like this:

PICTURE	SOUND
Details of movements by camera or within shot. Colours?	Details of sound: sound effects (FX), music; dialogue. You can mix these.
Shot no: 1 **MS** man's face at window. Light inside room. Window frame dark. Orange street light on man's face.	Wind FX
Shot no: 2 **VLS** dark street. An orange street light. Black car comes round corner R. Headlamps light up houses opposite.	Wind FX. Faint car engine FX, getting louder as car rounds the corner. Dog bark FX.

Pictures In the Mind

The Garden of Love

I went to the Garden of Love,
And saw what I never had seen;
A Chapel was built in the midst,
Where I used to play on the green.

And the gates of this Chapel were shut,
And 'Thou shalt not' writ over the door;
So I turn'd to the Garden of Love
That so many sweet flowers bore;

And I saw it was filled with graves,
And tomb-stones where flowers should be;
And Priests in black gowns were walking their rounds
And binding with briars my joys and desires.

William Blake

Leading in

We don't just accept the things that we 'see' in poems and pictures. Poets and artists choose and place images which our imaginations can link to our memories, thoughts and feelings. For instance, reference to the setting sun in a poem may cause us to feel sad or tired or restful. What we feel about such an image will depend on which of our memories, experiences and associations are called upon as we read and think about the whole poem.

Blake's poem expects us to use our imagination. Read it through again to see what pictures and feelings it conjures up in your mind.

Thinking about the poem

1 Often we use language to share our responses to a poem. This time, don't. Have some time to yourself. Concentrate on the imagery – the picture or pictures that you see in the poem.

2 When you are ready, sketch what you have seen in the poem. You might want to draw one sketch or several; you might want to draw realistically or in some other style. Trust your imagination as you create a *visual* response to the poem and its imagery. This is a chance to let your mind think and feel without having to rely on words.

3 Now share this visual response with a partner. Using your pictures, explain to each other what you have seen in the poem and identify which words, phrases or lines caused you to have these images. Where in the poem are your images (what you have seen) similar to those of your partner? Where are they different? Use the poem to help you justify your views.

Coursework ideas

(*e l*) 1 Write an account of what you have drawn and done, basing your account on these three stages:

Using your illustrations to help you, write about the images and thoughts and feelings you found at first in the poem.

Describe how your ideas were altered or reinforced when you discussed them and the poem with your partner.

Comment on how you feel about the poem now.

(Throughout, remember to use the poem and your illustrations to support what you wish to say. Quote from the poem and include your sketches at appropriate points in your written work.)

(*e*) 2 Write a story, a description or another poem which uses some of the images you have found in 'The Garden of Love'.

(*e l*) 3 Find three poems which appeal strongly to sight. Find or create one or more illustrations which could accompany them in an illustrated poetry anthology. Present your choice of poems and illustrations with an explanation of your choices.

Signposts Poems which could link with coursework assignments are 17, 32, 48, 53, 55, 63.

Sense Abilities

Fishing harbour towards evening

Slashed clouds leak gold. Along the slurping wharf
The snugged boats creak and seesaw. Round the masts

Abrasive squalls flake seagulls off the sky:
Choppy with wings the rapids of shrill sound.

Wrapt in spliced airs of fish and tar,
Light wincing on their knives, the clockwork men

Incise and scoop the oily pouches, flip
The soft guts overboard with blood-wet fingers.

Among three rhythms the slapping silver turns
To polished icy marble upon the deck.

Richard Kell

32

Leading in

In art lessons, you probably have to draw from life. You need to be observant and use your pencil skilfully to get shapes and sizes true to life. As you improve, you use shading to suggest texture, perhaps the firm curved smoothness of an apple or the rough jagged feel of a stone. If you use paint, you can use colour to build up a sense of three dimensions and to suggest texture. A skilful visual artist can even suggest movement to someone looking at the picture.

'Word artists' – poets – are also observant. The words they use can set off many kinds of sense experience for an alert reader.

Richard Kell has packed the lines of his description of an evening scene with a variety of sense experiences.

Thinking about the poem

1 Draw five columns on a sheet of paper and head each column **Sight**, **Sound**, **Touch**, **Taste** and **Smell**. (You will need this for some shared work and then for some work on your own.)

2 Work with a partner. Read the first four lines again. Discuss and note down particular words or phrases which cause you to experience the scene through one, or more than one, of your senses. For example, 'creak' could go in your sound column. What about 'seesaw'? Is it a sound or a movement (sight column) or both?

3 When you have done this for the first four lines, compare the notes on your chart with somebody else's. Concentrate on your differences of opinion.

4 Now complete this 'sense hunt' through the rest of the poem on your own.

Coursework ideas

1 Choose the words or phrases in this poem which give you the most precise and memorable sense experiences. (Between five and ten will do.) Quote each of these and underneath it comment on the senses it relies upon, for example:

   Abrasive squalls flake seagulls off the sky

   This appeals to the sense of sight. I get the impression of seagulls as dirty white and as small as bits of paint coming off a ceiling. They don't just drop. The wind scrapes them off, so that means there's touch here as well.

2 Choose another poem which appeals strongly to your senses and try out this approach again.

 Poems which could link themselves with coursework assignments are 13, 16, 20, 49, 55.

Sounds and Moods

Purpose: to investigate the part that sounds can play in creating our response to a poem.

Hospital Barge at Cérisy

Budging the sluggard ripples of the Somme,
A barge round old Cérisy slowly slewed.
Softly her engines down the current screwed
And chuckled in her, with contented hum.

Till fairy tinkling struck their croonings dumb.
The waters rumpling at the stern subdued.
The lock-gate took her bulging amplitude.
Gently from out the gurgling lock she swam.

One reading by that sunset raised his eyes
To watch her lessening westward quietly,
Till, as she neared the bend, her funnel screamed.

And that long lamentation made him wise
How unto Avalon, in agony,
Kings passed in the dark barge, which Merlin dreamed.

Wilfred Owen

Leading in

People talking about a film they've seen often say, 'What great photography!' but you rarely hear people say, 'I thought the sound effects were brilliant!'. Yet skilled men and women spend hundreds of hours recording, mixing and balancing sound effects with music and dialogue to produce an overall sound track. Some film sound may be used for dramatic effect, for atmosphere, or to help us believe that what we see is really happening. Sometimes, the sound carries more meaning than the picture.

Many poems may seem 'visual' like a film and, like a film, rely on skilful use of sounds to make their full impact. For example, Wilfred Owen was a poet who used words particularly skilfully to catch sound and use it for dramatic effect. He wrote many poems about the First World War, including this one about a hospital barge carrying the wounded down the River Somme and away from the trenches.

Thinking about the poem

1 On your own, or with a partner, make a note of words at the end of lines that rhyme.

2 Now, look closely at the poem again, starting to hunt for other places where sounds get repeated. Jot down:

   sounds repeated at the beginnings of words, e.g. '*sl*uggard'   '*sl*ewed';

   sounds repeated at the ends of words, e.g. 'rumpl*ing*'   'bulg*ing*';

   sounds repeated, regardless of where they appear: '*S*omme'   'Cé*ris*y'.

3 Compare your findings with those of others. Add to your list any other patterns of sounds you missed but agree with.

4 Look at your list again. Then re-read the poem, noticing the effect of patterns of sound. Which patterns of sound do you feel are 'sound effects', that is, sounds made by things happening in that river scene?

   On the left hand side of your sheet of rough paper, list each of the things you can hear making sounds in the poem. Alongside each, quote the words from the poem which catch and transmit that sound, for example:

   sound of the barge's clumsy bow   'Budging the sluggard ripples'.

   Compare your ideas with others' lists.

5 So far, you have been compiling evidence of how sound helps you to build the scene inside your head. It can do more than that. Patterns of sound can create a mood or atmosphere. What feeling(s) about the river does the poem evoke in its first half? What does the poem make you feel about the barge in the first ten lines? Write about these feelings freely, for about half a page. Then write about the feelings the last four lines summon up.

6 Share your findings with a partner. Discuss and jot down the patterns of sound which most affected your feelings. You could share your ideas with the rest of the class.

Coursework ideas

el 1 Taking line 11 as your start, write two more verses of this poem describing the barge as it continues its sad journey. (You could imagine this within the barge, if you wanted to.)

e 2 Find some photographs of the First World War. Write a commentary based on these. Your task is to evoke the sounds implied by the images they contain.

el 3 Write a piece, based on your lesson notes, about how Owen uses sound in this poem.

Signposts   A further poem which lends itself to this approach is 57.

Patterns In Poems

Purpose: to look for the pattern of rhythm and rhyme which can give a poem its form.

Leading in

The lim'rick's an odd sort of verse
With two rhymes in five lines which are terse.
It sets out to amuse
Or to mock or abuse
Or to shock or be downright perverse!

Mike Hayhoe

Some poems are written to a definite pattern. One of the most popular and most easily recognised patterns is that for the limerick. If it does not follow the rules of the pattern, the verse can't be a limerick. There are rules for the number and length of lines and for the rhyme and rhythm schemes. By tradition, limericks are not to be taken seriously – but they have to obey their rules.

Thinking about the limerick

1   Look at the following limerick:

The robes of the Vicar of Cheltenham	(a)
Gave pleasure whenever he knelt in 'em	(a)
But they got rather hot	(b)
When he wore them a lot	(b)
And the Vicar of Cheltenham smelt in 'em.	(a)

You will notice that
- a limerick has five lines
- lines 1, 2 and 5 have the same rhyme (a,a,a)
- lines 3 and 4 share another rhyme (b,b)
- the rhyme scheme is therefore aabba.

2   Count the syllables in each line and jot them down. Note how regular they are, with lines 1, 2 and 5 being long and 3 and 4 short.

3   With a partner, recite the limerick in a sing-song voice. Notice where you put stresses on syllables. Write out the limerick. Wherever a syllable is stressed,

put a ‾ above it and put a ⌣ above any unstressed syllable. The line 'The robes of the Vicar of Cheltenham' will look like this, for example:

⌣ ‾ ⌣ ⌣ ‾ ⌣ ⌣ ‾ ⌣
The robes of the Vicar of Cheltenham

Coursework idea

e

Try writing a poem of your own, using a particular verse form. You will find a limerick a good form to start with. Remember that you have to stick to the rules of the pattern: rhyme + line length + syllable count + stress patterns. To add further poems which use definite patterns, try one or more from the following *Verse Recipes*.

Verse recipes

Haiku

A Japanese verse form which looks simple but which expects you to suggest a lot in very few words.

- 3 lines
- Line I has 5 syllables
- Line 2 has 7 syllables
- Line 3 has 5 syllables
- no rhyme
- usually, written on an aspect of nature – creatures, seasons, weather, etc.
- uses one or two images to suggest a mood

> The fog steals all shapes
>   making this land a still sea,
>   casting us adrift.

Cinquain

A very brief European verse form which, like the haiku, expects you to suggest more than you can state. The first four lines build up. Experiment with the effects you can achieve in the last line.

- 5 lines
- Line I has I word or 2 syllables
- Line 2 has 2 words or 4 syllables
- Line 3 has 3 words or 6 syllables
- Line 4 has 4 words or 8 syllables
- Line 5 has I word or 2 syllables

Fog swims
around the lamps
of the oncoming bus.
The silver doors hiss open, close.
It's gone.

Diamante

A strictly controlled diamond-shaped poem which describes one thing for its first half in increasing detail until the middle of line 4. It then goes into reverse, describing something else until it is named at the end of the second half. This is handy for playing at contrasts, for example, day and night / cat and dog / youth and age / sorrow and joy.

- 7 lines
- Line I   Noun I
- Line 2   Adjective   Adjective
- Line 3   Verb + ing   Verb + ing   Verb + ing
- Line 4   Synonym Synonym / Start contrast here / Synonym Synonym
- Line 5   Verb + ing   Verb + ing   Verb + ing
- Line 6   Adjective   Adjective
- Line 7   Noun 2

Fog
sly   chill
creeping stealing puzzling
robber bereaver; comforter optimist
gliding climbing warming
gentle benevolent
Sun

Ballad

A good verse form for telling a tale. Most ballads used to tell of love, daring or infamous deeds. Some managed to get all those strands in one ballad.

- A series of verses – as many as the tale needs.
- Usually 4 lines to a verse.
- Usually some sort of rhyme, often lines 1 and 3 rhyming and lines 2 and 4 (rhyme scheme ABAB)
- A strong sense of rhythm, so that the words can be sung or have their own regular beat.

Dusk's fog ambushed the motorway
And yet there were the fools who raced
Head on into its formless grey
Until it was their deaths they faced.

Sonnet

An advanced verse form, often used to tell of the joys and sorrows of love, but other topics can benefit from the crossword puzzle it causes as you try to find words to suit your meaning and fit its rhythm and rhyme!

- 14 lines
- Each line has 10 syllables
- There are 5 pairs of syllables to a line ('pentameter')
- Each pair of syllables ('foot') uses a 'light' unstressed syllable, followed by a 'heavy' stressed syllable (an 'iambic foot') This pattern is called 'iambic pentameter' ʊ/ ʊ/ ʊ/ ʊ/ ʊ/.
- The Shakespearean sonnet has a rhyme scheme ABABCDCDEFEFGG.
- Think of the scheme as 3 quatrains (verse of four lines) and 1 couplet: ABAB CDCD EFEF GG. You can then try describing three aspects of something in the first three phases of your sonnet and use your couplet to round off the poem.

A first four lines might be something like this:

Sometimes the world seems clear and simplified
But there are times when all around is dull.
The mist and fog within myself provide
No joy, no sense of living to the full.

Making Words Echo

Purpose: to look at a poem and see how far it depends on rhyme to make it memorable and striking.

Hard Frost

Frost called to water 'Halt!'
And crushed the moist snow with sparkling salt;
Brooks, their own bridges, stop,
And icicles in long stalactites drop,
And tench in water-holes
Lurk under gluey glass like fish in bowls.

In the hard-rutted lane,
At every footstep breaks a brittle pane,
And tinkling trees ice-bound,
Changed into weeping willows, sweep the ground;
Dead boughs take root in ponds
And ferns on windows shoot their ghostly fronds.

But vainly the fierce frost
Interns poor fish, ranks trees in an armed host.
Hangs daggers from house-eaves
And on the windows ferny ambush weaves;
In the long war grown warmer
The sun will strike him dead and strip his armour.

Andrew Young

Leading in

Words which sound the same, or almost the same, are more likely to make us notice them than words which don't. There is something about words which 'echo' one another which makes us pay attention and helps us to 'hear' the poem.

Many poets use rhyme to let us know that we are reading a poem, not prose. They may use it for other reasons as well.

Thinking about the poem

1 Read the following notes:

End rhyme

In the first verse, the ends of the lines rhyme: halt/salt; stop/drop; water-holes/bowls. We would write that rhyme as a,a,b,b,**c,c** – the poem is in rhyming couplets.

End rhyme gives pleasure since sometimes we can guess what the rhyming word will be. Sometimes it is a surprise. Rhyme helps us to remember lines. A poet may draw attention to central ideas in the poem by placing key words in the rhyming slots. For example, 'Halt!' is a key word in a poem which is going to say a lot about winter bringing everything to a stop.

List the end rhymes for the second and third verses. Which of these seem to be especially important? Why?

Front rhyme

Another name for this is *alliteration* – where words start with the same sounds. In that first verse, for example, *b*rooks and *b*ridges, and *g*luey and *g*lass are linked by alliteration.

Make notes on the impression these word links give you.

Internal rhyme

Sometimes you may find words which make the same or a similar sound *inside* a line or verse. This poem has a few words which have a similar but not identical sound.

Look at the first two lines of the first verse and see how 'fr*o*st' and 'cr*u*sted' are linked by a similar sound.

2 With a partner, choose one of the two other verses where you think the end rhymes in the couplets are striking and point towards important ideas in the poem. Jot down these key words and why you think they are important to the poem.

If you have found one or two front rhymes or internal rhymes, do the same for these. Be prepared to share your notes with other pairs of students.

Coursework ideas

el **1** Show how rhymes have brought to your attention some of the main ideas and feelings in this poem about a winter world and its eventual defeat.

el **2** Find two or three other poems which deal with a time of year. Write an introduction for them which could be used in a poetry anthology or which could be used for a radio broadcast.

e **3** Write a poem on something which interests you, using rhyme. You can use all the types identified here – end rhyme, internal rhyme, front rhyme – or concentrate on just one. Present your drafts and the final version with a commentary on what you wanted to achieve, the problems you had, how far you managed to solve them and your opinion of the final version.

 Further poems which lend themselves to this approach are 16, 30, 39, 40, 54, 60.

Playing With the Rules

Purpose: to see how a poet can play with what appear to be strict rules controlling a poem.

Cats

Cats no less liquid than their shadows
Offer no angles to the wind.
They slip, diminished, neat, through loopholes
Less than themselves; will not be pinned

To rules or routes for journeys; counter
Attack with non-resistance; twist
Enticing through the curving fingers
And leave an angered, empty fist.

They wait obsequious as darkness
Quick to retire, quick to return;
Admit no aim or ethics; flatter
With reservations; will not learn

To answer to their names; are seldom
Truly owned till shot or skinned.
Cats, no less liquid than their shadows
Offer no angles to the wind.

A.S.J. Tessimond

Leading in

One of the advantages poets have is that they can choose a set of rules – and play around with them. They might decide to set out a poem in what *seem* to be regular verses, with a regular rhyme scheme, so that casual readers feel that they know what to expect. But they might be mistaken. Alert readers should be able to spot where the poet has played with the rules, and ask themselves why. Sometimes, reading a poem aloud shows you that the poet is playing tricks. For instance, A.S.J. Tessimond was rather good at playing with the rules to create a sense of surprise.

Thinking about the poem

1 Try out different ways of reading the poem. First of all, see what happens if you stop at the end of every line as if each line were a sentence! Then look at the punctuation and read the poem again. Finally, prepare a reading which best shows your understanding of the poem.

2 In a group of up to four people, prepare a reading script of the poem which uses all your voices.

   You could use these symbols:

   / = brief pause
   // = long pause
   −− = keep moving
   p = soft voice
   f = strong voice

If you need more, make up your own.

Perform a reading of your poem. (This might be used as part of your GCSE oral assessment.)

Coursework ideas

1 What else makes Tessimond's poem a 'cat' poem? Look at how the poem uses negative words – cats won't do as they are told! Look at sounds. Look at how the lines move, as well as at movement words. Write, as if to a twelve year old pupil, an explanation of what this poem is about and how it achieves its effect.

2 Find one or two other poems about cats. Bearing in mind your work on Tessimond's poem, write an essay explaining how the poets have helped you to create the cats in your mind.

Further poems which lend themselves to this approach are 6, 16, 24, 34.

Poems which could link with coursework assignments are 15, 16, 70.

Attempting the Impossible

Purpose: to ask you to share the problems of a translator in trying to retain the features of a poem as you put it into a new language.

This is one of the earliest protests against noise pollution. Someone from six hundred years ago is fed up with the blacksmiths working night shift next door!

The Blacksmiths

Swarte smekyd smethes smateryd wyth smoke
Dryve me to deth wyth den of here dyntes.
Swech noys on nyghts ne herd men never:
What knavene cry and clateryng of knockes!
The cammede kongons cryen after 'col! col!'
And blowen there bellewys, that al here brayn brestes.
'Huf, puf!' seith that on. 'Haf, paf!' that other.
Thei spyttyn and spraulyn and spellen many spelles.
Thei gnauen and gnacchen, theie gronys togydere
And holdyn hem hote wyth here hard hamers.
Of a bole-hyde ben here barm-fellys.
Here schankes ben schakeled for the fere-flunderys.
Hevy hamerys thei han, that hard ben handled,
Stark strokes thei stryken on a stelyd stokke:
Lus, bus! las, das! rowtyn be rowe.
Sweche dolful a dreme the devyl it todryve!
The mayster longith a lityl, and lasceth a lesse,
Twyneth hem tweyn, and towchith a treble:
Tik, tak! hic, hac! tiket, taket! tyk, tak!
Lus, bus! lus, das! swych lyf thei ledyn
Alle clothemerys. Cryst hem gyve sorwe!
May no man for branwaterys on nyght han hys rest!

Anon
(About 1425–1450)

Leading in

There is no such thing as a completely faithful translation of a poem. Translating from another language into English inevitably changes the meaning. The same applies when we translate an old poem into current language. And yet we try, because some poems from other times and cultures are too good to miss. Here is a very literal prose translation of the poem:

> Smoke-blackened smiths, begrimed with smoke, drive me to death with the noise of their strokes. Such noise at night nobody ever heard – such calling out by servants and clattering of blows! The snub-nosed changelings call for 'Coal! Coal!' and inflate their bellows so that all their brain bursts. 'Huff, Puff!' says that one, 'Haff, Paff!' another. They spit and move in an ungainly fashion and tell many tales. They grind and gnash their teeth, they complain together and keep themselves hot with their hard hammerings. Of bull-hide are their aprons made. Their legs are protected against fiery sparks. They have heavy hammers that are handled strongly. Hard strokes they strike on an anvil made of steel – 'Lus, bus! Las, das!' they beat in turn. So doleful a noise would destroy the Devil. The master lengthens a short piece of iron and beats out a smaller, joins them together and hits a treble note (on the anvil). 'Tik, tak! Hic, hac! Tiket, taket! Tik, tak! Lus, bus! Las, das!' Such a life they lead, all mare-dressers (i.e. putting armour on horses). May Christ give them sorrow! No man, because of the water-burners, can at night get his rest!

Thinking about the poem

1 Read the poem again in both versions.

2 With a partner decide on any bits in the prose translation which start to capture the noise of the smithy and the mood of the sleepless protester.

3 With your partner, produce a translation of at least five lines of the poem as a poem. (Try to use the layout of the original poem.) Remember that you are trying to use modern language to create the sounds and pictures and, much more important, the mood of the original poem.

4 Share your work with other pairs. See how far they have achieved the sounds, pictures and mood of the original.

Coursework ideas

e l 1 Produce a translation of the complete poem, remembering that you are trying to create the sounds, pictures and moods of the original poem in modern English. Then write a commentary on any problems you met and whether you think you managed to solve them.

e l 2 If you are studying a foreign language, find a poem in that language. Produce, with help if necessary, a literal prose version of the poem. Then create your own more poetic version in English. Comment on the problems you faced and how you solved them.

Fake a Blake

from 'Auguries of Innocence'

A Robin Redbreast in a cage
Puts all Heaven in a rage.

A Dove house filled with Doves and Pigeons
Shudders hell through all its regions.

A Dog starved at his master's gate
Predicts the ruin of the state.

A Horse misused upon the road
Calls to Heaven for human blood.

Each outcry of the hunted Hare
A fibre from the brain does tear.

A Skylark wounded in the wing,
A cherubin does cease to sing.

The Game Cock clipped and armed for fight
Does the rising sun affright.

William Blake

Leading in

We all like watching and listening to a skilled impressionist 'taking off' somebody. We enjoy how impressionists imitate their victims so that:

- they *look* and *sound* similar in build, height, facial features, ways of moving, voices and ways of speaking
- they have similar *views* on similar *topics*
- they have similar *temperaments*.

Just as impressionists gain a great deal through working at imitiating others, we can learn a lot about a poem by writing verses which aim to be like the original poem in as many ways as possible. That means paying attention to what the original poem looks and sounds like, what it is interested in and what it feels about this topic.

Thinking about the poem

1 With a partner, read the extract again. Make brief notes about each couplet (pair of lines) under the following headings: **Looks and Sounds, Topics, Feelings**. Note any topics or feelings which appear in more than one couplet.

2 Use your notes to make a list of guidelines on how to write couplets as much like Blake's as possible.

3 Check your guidelines with some made by other pairs. If you think that you have missed out anything important, add it to your list.

4 Use your revised guidelines to compose further couplets with your partner or on your own.

Coursework ideas

 1 Find a poem in the anthology which also has a strong pattern involving rhyme and rhythm.

Write a set of guidelines on this new poem for your own use. (**Looks** and **Sounds, Topics, Feelings**).

Write further verses as much like the original as possible.

Under your version, write a piece in which you explain all the ways in which it is like, and unlike, the original poem. (You could use this piece of writing as part of a unit or as a whole one. Whichever you choose to do, make sure that you include an extract from the original poem.)

 2 Find other poems in the anthology which express protest and anger. Explain what causes the mood in the poem and how the poet gets you to share these feelings.

Further poems which lend themselves to this approach are 8, 18, 54, 56, 65.

Poems which could link with coursework assignments are 2, 22, 31, 39, 40, 50, 76.

Will the Real Poem Please Stand Up?

Purpose: to explore the difficulties of choice that a poet may have.

Leading in

A poet called Samuel Taylor Coleridge once said that poetry is 'the best words in the best order'. Whether you agree with that or not, poets do try to be careful and to craft what they have to say. They have to make choices, for example, what form the poem should take, whether it should rhyme or not, which words to use. The lines printed opposite show the problems of choice that one writer faced in finding the 'best' words for what he wanted to convey. The poem has been printed to show the places where he had difficult decisions to make. Which word gets on better with its neighbours?

Thinking about the poem

1 On your own, jot down the word which you would have chosen at each problem point.

2 With a partner, work through your choices, seeing where you agree and disagree.

3 Discuss and make notes on what you and your partner feel are the different meanings suggested by the two versions of a line. For instance, what do you think are the differences between the sheet of paper being 'followed' by a coke can rather than 'chased' by it?

Coursework ideas

el 1 Write out the version which you would be prepared to defend. Write a commentary, explaining why you chose the option you did at each problem point and why you rejected its alternative.

o 2 Present your choice and reasons to others. This can be a good opportunity for GCSE oral communication coursework.

City Blues

Sunday dawn in a November city

the bully ⟨light / sun⟩ wades in

sets glass aflame

⟨slams / puts⟩ ⟨dark / hard⟩ shadows on anything

not big enough to take it.

The wind ⟨strips / unzips⟩ trees

makes them tittletattle

harsh small talk

⟨puts / drives⟩ their leaves into a lurch

somewhere.

A sheet of paper

⟨followed / chased⟩ by a coke can

takes ridiculously to the air

⟨floats / flaps⟩ into the sunlight

is a ⟨swan / bird⟩

tumbles

knows its place

as the less fortunate should.

In the ⟨shadow / shade⟩

this ⟨miniscule / small⟩ steeple

comes to the point

which is more than can be said

for the big-time ⟨corporations / companies⟩

and their ⟨skyscrapers / sky-spoilers⟩

⟨napalmed / lit up⟩ by that

lousy sun.

Mike Hayhoe

The Problem of Choosing

Purpose: to experience some of the dilemmas a poet might encounter when writing a poem.

Leading in

A poet faces several problems in writing a poem. One of them is choosing the language and shape to fit what needs to be said. Here, the basic ideas from an actual poem have been written out as prose. Read this prose version carefully, because the aim is to make it come alive again as a poem. You will not write the poem that the poet did, but that does not matter. You and your partner will experience some of the challenges that the poet faced.

A CAT

The children knew her name, but nobody loved her, although somebody was her owner. That person locked her out when it was time for bed and had her kittens drowned when they were born.

When it was Springtime, this cat ate birds – blackbirds, thrushes and nightingales. She ate birds which were bright in all sorts of ways – in their song, their colours and their flight. And she ate scraps from the neighbours' waste.

The poet detested, hated the cat for this, for a single marking on the breast of a thrush was worth a million such cats as this one – and yet she lived many years, until God provided her with rest.

Thinking about the poem

1 This prose may carry the ideas and feeling that the poet had, but it is not doing very well! Read it again and try to imagine what the poet felt about the cat, how the creature is treated and how it treats others.

2 With a partner try to write the poem. You should use the poem's original title – 'A Cat'. As far as you can, try to follow the original poem's shape. To do this, turn each of the blocks of prose into a verse of four lines. In each verse, lines two and four rhyme, but lines one and three do not.

3 Now, with your partner, compare your poem with the original (see page 70). See how far the poet's choices of language and shape were similar to yours.

Coursework ideas

(*e l*) 1 Write a copy of the original poem alongside your own. Then compare the things you and the poet talked about, what you and the poet felt about them, the language you and the poet used, the shapes (verse form, rhyme, metre, length of lines) that you and the poet chose.

(*o*) 2 Using your notes from Coursework Idea 1, with your partner prepare a reading of your poem and a brief talk. Explain how your poem is like or unlike the original in what you chose to describe and how you described it.

(*e*) 3 Write a prose description of a creature or an event and then write a poem on the same topic, using the same material. Explain which you prefer.

The Early Bird Counts Its Chickens

Purpose: to explore figurative language through a study of proverbs.

Proverbs

A lie has short legs.

You need a lot of spades to bury truth.

When your enemy is an ant, fear him like a lion.

Sit crooked, but talk straight.

You can't block out the sun with your hand.

If there were no wind, cobwebs would cover the sky.

When it thunders, each man is afraid of himself.

Even the sun goes through mud, but it doesn't get dirty.

He gets in your eyes like sweat.

A wolf pays with his skin.

Measure a wolf's tail when he's dead.

Even his tail is a burden to a tired fox.

Vasco Popa
Translated by Anne Pennington

Leading in

In the days when most people were not taught to read, older people often passed on wisdom and advice in the form of 'mini-poems' called proverbs. It was important that these proverbs were easy to remember. Some proverbs were memorable because they rhymed:

There's many a slip
'Twixt the cup and the lip

or because of repeated sounds at the start of words (alliteration):

Look before you leap.

The meaning of some proverbs was very straightforward:

A fool and his money are soon parted.

Others used everyday situations which young listeners would have experienced for themselves, such as:

The early bird catches the worm

and

Don't count your chickens before they're hatched.

Thinking about the poem

1 Decide on two of these proverbs that specially strike you. Share your choice with a partner and discuss the wisdom or advice that you feel they contain.

2 In larger groups or with the whole class, share your ideas about as many as you can.

3 The poem may look like a list of individual proverbs, but if you look closely you can probably notice different kinds of connections. For example, fierce animals are mentioned in four of them. Perhaps you feel that some of these proverbs contradict each other. With a partner, make notes about any connections and contradictions you can see.

Coursework ideas

1 Choose the proverb which has interested you most. Use it as a title and write your own story or playscript which illustrates its meaning.

2 Using your lesson notes as a starting point, write a piece which explores the meanings of the individual proverbs in the poem. If you found connections or contradictions or think a theme is developed in the poem, write about this as well.

How Simple Is Simple?

Purpose: to explore the deeper meanings which lie beneath an apparently simple, childlike poem.

Anger's Freeing Power

I had a dream three walls stood up wherein a raven bird
Against the walls did beat himself and was not this absurd?

For the sun and rain beat in that cell that had its fourth wall free
And daily blew the summer shower and the rain came presently

And all the pretty summer time and all the winter too
That foolish bird did beat himself till he was black and blue.

Rouse up, rouse up, my raven bird, fly by the open wall
You make a prison of a place that is not one at all.

I took my raven by the hand, Oh come, I said, my Raven,
And I will take you by the hand and you shall fly to heaven.

But oh he sobbed and oh he sighed and in a fit he lay
Until two fellow ravens came and stood outside to say:

You wretched bird, conceited lump
You well deserve to pine and thump.

See now a wonder, mark it well
My bird rears up in angry spell,

Oh do I then? he says, and careless flies
O'er flattened wall at once to heaven's skies.

And in my dream I watched him go
And I was glad, I loved him so,

Yet when I woke my eyes were wet
To think Love had not freed my pet,

Anger it was that won him hence
As only Anger taught him sense.

Often my tears fall in a shower
Because of Anger's freeing power.

Stevie Smith

54

Leading in

A fable is an old form of story which depends for its effect on a simple story line, followed by clear advice on one aspect of life and how to live it.

Thinking about the poem

1 Look for anything in the poem which seems to be more for young children than for adults. Jot down your ideas. With a partner, produce a list you agree on.

2 People have always used animals as *emblems* (e.g. ant = industriousness, elephant = long memory) and as characters in *fables*. This poem is like many fables in that its uses an animal. What does the raven stand for here?

3 This is a 'dream poem'. One dictionary says a dream is 'a train of thoughts, images or fancies passing through the mind during sleep'.

   For thousands of years, people have felt that dreams are important and have meanings. With your partner, work out an interpretation of this poem and note down your ideas.

4 What title(s) would you choose to fit your interpretation of the dream?

   Write down why you think Stevie Smith chose her title.

5 Some might see this poem as a simple fable; some as a strange dream; some as a mixture. As you read it again, do your views change?

Coursework ideas

e 1 Write a fable in prose or verse with your advice on anger, which could be read to a young child.

e 2 Write a piece of prose or poetry entitled 'Dream'. If you wish, you can use the images and unusual trains of thought of your own dreams.

e l 3 Write about how you see this poem. Is it a fable, a dream or a mixture? Is it a poem for young children? Support your views with evidence from the poem and your notes.

e l 4 This poem raises issues about anger. Find another poem which explores this emotion. Write about similarities and differences you find and about anything else which seems significant to you.

 **Signposts**

Further poems which lend themselves to this approach are 18, 23.

Poems which could link with coursework assignments are 1, 5, 41.

It's the Same Old Story

> **Purpose:** to get you to look for the stories behind the main events in a narrative poem.

John Hardy

John Hardy was a brave and a desperate boy,
Said he carried two guns every day.
He shot him a man in the Shawnee camp,
And I seen John gettin' away, poor boy!
And I seen John Hardy gettin' away.

John Hardy had a little lovin' wife,
And children he had three,
But he cared no more for his wife and babes,
Than he cared for the rocks in the sea, poor boy!
Than he cared for the rocks in the sea.

John Hardy was a-standin' by the dark sea bar,
He was unconcerned in the game,
Up stepped a yaller girl with twenty dollars in her hand,
Said: 'Deal John Hardy in the game, poor boy!'
Said: 'Deal John Hardy in the game.'

John Hardy stepped up with the money in his hand,
Sayin': 'I have money for to play,
And the one who wins this yaller girl's dough,
I have powder to blow him away, poor boy!
I have powder to blow him away!

The cards was dealt and the money on the board.
Dave Campbell won that twenty dollar bill.
John Hardy drew his pistol and took sure aim and fired,
And he caused Dave Campbell's brains to spill, poor boy!
And he caused Dave Campbell's brains to spill.

John Hardy had twelve mile to go
And six of them he ran.
He ran, he came to the river bank,
Then he fell on his bosom and he swam, poor boy!
Then he fell on his bosom and he swam.

John Hardy went to this big long town,
And he thought he was out of the way.
Up stepped a marshal and took him by the hand,
Says: 'John Hardy, come and go with me, poor boy!'
Says: 'John Hardy, come and go with me.'

John Hardy's wife was dressed in blue.
She came for to go his bail.
No bail was allowed for murderin' a man,
So they put John Hardy back in jail, poor boy!
So they put John Hardy back in jail.

John Hardy stood in the middle of his cell,
And the tears run down his eyes,
Says: 'I've been the death of many a man
And now I am ready for to die, poor boy!
And now I am ready for to die.

I've been to the East, I've been to the West,
I've travelled this wide world round,
I've been down to the river and I've been baptized,
So take me to the hangin' ground, poor boy!
So take me to the hangin' ground.'

Anon

Leading in

Throughout the ages, stories have been told in poetry. Many of these poems
were (and are) sung or spoken aloud, often with musical accompaniment. Many of
the stories were told over and over again, until only the 'best bits' were left in –
the singers had to tell a good yarn if they were to catch and keep an audience.

Thinking about the poem

1 With a partner, sort out and note down the story line. Thinking of *Who? Where?
   When? Why? What?* as you tackle each verse can be helpful. For example, who
   are the main characters and where does the action take place? You will
   sometimes have to 'read between the lines'.

2 The passage on the next page, **Bad Loser Hits Rock Bottom** shows how a
   newspaper might have written the story of John Hardy. Read it and list any
   similarities it shares with the poem.

BAD LOSER HITS ROCK BOTTOM
Judge Sentences Hardy to Hang

John Edward Hardy, aged 35, unemployed former horse-dealer, was yesterday sentenced to hang for the murder of David Campbell, 30, in the Golden Nugget Bar, Dansville. Sentencing him to death, Judge Warren Johnson described Hardy as 'a pathetic waster, who had squandered his opportunities and abused the loyalty and love of his devoted wife and children.'

Loyal Wife In Tears

His attractive wife, Lucy Hardy, collapsed in tears at the verdict. 'I would have done anything to help him,' she told reporters. As she comforted her children, she admitted that her ten-year marriage to Hardy had been difficult. 'John found it difficult to settle. He'd led such an eventful life before we met.'

Point Blank End To Disastrous Evening

Hardy shot Campbell at point blank range, following an argument over a game of cards at the Golden Nugget. Some witnesses spoke of a young woman, who lent Hardy some money to continue gambling after he had lost all his. She was not available to give evidence at the trial.

Error Of His Ways

According to Dean Cartwright, the town jailor, Hardy spoke often of his regret at his wasted life. He had apparently killed before, though he had not been tried for any of these alleged killings, according to State records. The Reverend Wilbur Smith was later summoned to the jail house, where Hardy is to be held until his day of execution, fixed for Friday at noon.

---

3 Now look for and list any *differences* between the poem and the newspaper article. These might include:

what seems to have interested the writers
the order of events
how the story is divided up
types of language used
your feelings about the characters

4 The next piece is the opening extract from a short story about John Hardy.

Chapter 1

He had to get back. His thoughts were racing but, wherever they ran, they ended up at the same point: he had to get back.

The night air was cool on his face as he galloped. John was shivering. From fear or cold, it made little difference. After what he'd done, there was only one place to go. Home. A strange thought. Only six hours earlier, he'd left it, furious and frustrated. . .

'Dad, tell us a story.'

Nancy Hardy looked at her father pleadingly. Since that blazing row between her parents earlier that day, her father had sat motionless in the battered chair in the parlour, staring at the fire. It was nearly out now. Among the grey ashes a few logs smouldered at their edges. His face was drawn and grey. He didn't seem to have heard her.

She turned away. Outside the window, the sky showed dusk. Her younger brother appeared at the door carrying a pile of logs. Ben glanced at his father, then moved shyly across the room and dropped the logs awkwardly at the hearth.

As the children placed logs carefully on the fire to coax some life back into it, John Hardy stirred.

Nancy tried again.

'Tell us one of your stories, the one about that fight in the Swanee camp.' She smiled, rather desperately, at her father.

'I'll do that!' John shouted suddenly, falling to his knees and grabbing a log from Ben. They were the first words he'd spoken for hours.

'Aw, Paw. Let me!' Ben wailed. 'I ain't a baby. I can chop wood and fetch the water. Ma said I'm getting to be a reg'lar little man. . .

He stopped. His father's face had clouded, screwed into a rage too tight for words.

It was then that John had left.

A jolt brought him back to his senses. His horse's rhythmic movement was slowing awkwardly. It had gone lame. He cursed and dismounted. He was aware of his surroundings for the first time since he had galloped out of Dansville. He was at the fork in the road, still six miles from home . . . home and safety. The thought struck him as odd.

5 Look back at your notes. Discuss the way a narrative poem like 'John Hardy' tells its story. Is a narrative poem more like a newspaper article or like a short story?

Coursework ideas

e 1 Write the story, making John Hardy's wife the main character. She can tell her story or another character in the poem can tell it.

e 2 Write your own version of the John Hardy Story as a piece of prose or as a drama script. You may choose to concentrate on one small scene.

e 3 Choose a dramatic, 'human interest' story from a newspaper. Write your own narrative poem based on this. Use five line verses with a repeat on the last two lines, as in 'John Hardy'.

You could make a full coursework unit by writing a short story version of the original newspaper report. Present your poem, story and the newspaper cutting.

 Further poems which lend themselves to this approach are 26, 28, 31.

Points of View

Purpose: to investigate a poem in order to see that it can suggest more than one viewpoint.

The Mysterious Naked Man

A mysterious naked man has been reported
on Cranston Avenue. The police are performing
the usual ceremonies with coloured lights and sirens.
Almost everyone is outdoors and strangers are conversing excitedly
as they do during disasters when their involvement is peripheral.
"What did he look like?" the lieutenant is asking.
"I don't know," says the witness. "He was naked."
There is talk of dogs – this is no ordinary case
of indecent exposure, the man has been seen
a dozen times since the milkman spotted him and now
the sky is turning purple and voices
carry a long way and the children
have gone a little crazy as they often do at dusk
and cars are arriving
from other sections of the city.
And the mysterious naked man
is kneeling behind a garbage can or lying on his belly
in somebody's garden
or maybe even hiding in the branches of a tree,
where the wind from the harbour
whips at his naked body,
and by now he's probably done
whatever it was he wanted to do
and wishes he could go to sleep
or die
or take to the air like Superman.

Alden Nowlan

Leading in

Television and radio news have made us used to hearing several people give their opinions about a person or an incident. Here, a poet has shown us how various people react to the same 'newsworthy' event.

Thinking about the poem

1 Read the poem again, jotting down all the different people it mentions.

2 Check your list with a partner. Discuss what the various people would feel about the incident and how they would talk about it.

3 If you had been there, you might have overheard:

a statement by the lieutenant as the reporters pester him for details

the talk of two strangers who are 'conversing excitedly'

the interview of the witness by press and television reporters

the chatter of two children who have seen nothing but are excited by all the commotion.

With your partner, write the playscript of one of these conversations.

4 Exchange scripts so that you have a chance to read at least one other conversation. Jot down your opinions of the way each person talks about the incident.

5 Draw a line down the middle of your page. On the left-hand side, write down in your own words what you think the poet feels about the following people: the lieutenant, the excited strangers, the witness, the over-excited children, the mysterious naked man.

On the right-hand side, opposite each comment, jot down 'the clues' – the words, phrases or lines which helped you to decide what the poet feels about these people and their views.

Coursework ideas

el 1 Write the newspaper report of the incident, including quotations from bystanders you have interviewed.

o 2 Produce and tape the local radio report of the incident, using interviews.

el 3 Write what this poem helps you to understand about its main character and about people's reactions to misfits.

l 4 Write about how the misfit is viewed in this poem, compared with how misfits have been portrayed in other poems, plays or stories you have read.

Further poems which lend themselves to this approach are 26, 31, 76.

Poems which could link with coursework assignments are 14, 22, 43, 45, 52.

Reading Between the Lines

Fifteen

South of the bridge on Seventeenth
I found back of the willows one summer
day a motorcycle with engine running
as it lay on its side, ticking over
slowly in the high grass. I was fifteen.

I admired all that pulsing gleam, and
shiny flanks, the demure headlights
fringed where it lay; I led it gently
to the road and stood with that
companion, ready and friendly. I was fifteen.

We could find the end of a road, meet
the sky on out Seventeenth. I thought about
hills, and patting the handle got back a
confident opinion. On the bridge we indulged
a forward feeling, a tremble. I was fifteen.

Thinking, back further in the grass I found
the owner, just coming to, where he had flipped
over the rail. He had blood on his hand, was pale –
I helped him walk to his machine. He ran his hand
over it, called me good man, roared away.

I stood there, fifteen.

William Stafford

Leading in

People of all ages have found that poetry is a very good way of writing to explore their feelings. Sometimes they will state their feelings directly. Sometimes, their feelings may be less obvious, be only implied. For example, a writer could *state* a mood with the words 'I was embarrassed' and could *imply* the same embarrassment with 'I blushed and looked away.'

Thinking about the poem

1 Make three vertical columns on a sheet of paper and head them **Main feeling**, **Stated** and **Implied**.

2 Look again at the first verse. What do you sense is the main feeling about the incident it describes? Describe it briefly in the **Main feeling** column. If this feeling is stated, write down the words which do this in the **Stated** column. If the feeling is implied by any words in the first verse, quote them in the **Implied** column.

   When you've done this, compare your findings with a partner's.

3 On your own or in pairs, look at one verse at a time, thinking carefully and recording your impressions and findings in the same way as you did for the first verse.

4 You will have noticed that the chorus 'I was fifteen' appears at the end of each of the first three verses. Now that you have explored the poem, each repetition of this line will probably have a fuller meaning for you than it did when you first read it. Read the poem once more and write freely about the thoughts and feelings you now get as you read each 'I was fifteen'.

5 The last line of the poem is very clearly separated from the rest of it. Why do you think the poet chose to place it there on its own? What thoughts and feelings does it stir in you? Jot these down.

6 You could share your ideas in small groups or as a whole class.

Coursework ideas

e   1 Write an autobiographical piece in prose or poetry to show an incident in your past life which confused you at the time or which has had a lasting effect on the way that you think or feel. Use plenty of sense details to recreate that past incident, as well as exploring your thoughts and feelings.

e   2 Write your own poem which ends with the line 'I stood there, fifteen' (or any other age).

e l   3 Write a piece based on your lesson notes, which examines the various feelings presented in this poem and the ways the poet shows these, through the words chosen and the shape of the poem.

e l   4 Find other poems about childhood or adolescence and write a piece which explores the various feelings they contain.

Further poems which lend themselves to this approach are 4, 29, 51, 57, 59.

Poems which could link with coursework assignments are 5, 19, 22, 43, 44, 51.

Making Sound Sense

It's Going to Rain

It's going to rain,
says God to himself, yawning
as he looks at the sky in which
not the tiniest cloud is visible.
These forty days, forty nights
my rheumatism has been playing me up.
Yes, there's a downpour coming.

Noah, hey there, Noah,
come to the fence,
there's something I want to tell you.

Marin Sorescu
Translated by Michael Hamburger

Leading in

The way we say something often affects its meaning. The words we stress and the
tone of voice we use make a big difference. You could put a stress on one word
and affect the meaning, – 'These books are *quite* interesting' – and by the tone of
your voice as you said that you could be encouraging, pleasant or downright
sneering. Try speaking that sentence, using different tones and stressing
different words.

This approach to poetry looks at how we can express our understanding of a
poem's moods and attitudes by the way that we say the words. This poem is a
modern one, but it is based on the Old Testament story of the Flood, when God
destroyed almost every creature on Earth because of Man's evil. Try speaking the
following words to your partner in the style of the Old Testament God who was
angry and disappointed, but had one glimmer of hope and affection because of
the good man, Noah.

> And God saw that the wickedness of man was great in the earth . . . And the
> Lord said, I will destroy both man, and beast, and the creeping thing, and the
> fowls of the air, for it repenteth me that I have made them. But Noah found
> grace in the eyes of the Lord.

Thinking about the poem

1 What sort of God is this? How could your voice portray him to others? Make some notes on how you would want to read this poem. Find a quiet spot where you can read the poem to yourself until you are satisfied with your version of the poem and your notes on how to read it.

2 Share your ideas with a team of two or three others. Read out your version of the poem and listen to each of the others. Make notes about any bits of readings which you particularly liked and tell each reader at the end of her/his reading about them. Keep notes about what others liked about the readings.

3 Decide as a group who has the most *appropriate* voice for the poem.

4 Quickly make a copy of the poem, using alternate lines on the paper. On the blank lines, write instructions indicating the best way to read the lines. Try to include as many of the items that you liked from the previous readings, so that the final reading will pool everyone's ideas.

   Consider the following when writing your instructions:

   Volume – Do some bits need to be read more loudly / softly than others?

   Tone of voice – Will you use the same tone of voice all through? Will you, for example, need to sound angry, amused, sarcastic, sad, etc.?

   Pace – Will some parts need to be read faster or slower than others? What about pauses? Where will these occur?

5 Now rehearse your reader, using the reading script. Your reader will be asked to read your group's version of the poem to the rest of the class and the rest of the team will be asked to explain why they wanted that particular interpretation of the poem.

Coursework ideas

(el) 1 Find another poem which you think repays being read out loud. Produce the reading script for it and write your explanation of it.

(o) 2 As a member of a small team, produce a reading script for a poem which can use more than one voice. You might want one voice with the others as a chorus, or voices in unison. You might want sound effects or some background music. Make a live or taped presentation of your poem, with a live or taped commentary.

 Poems which could link with coursework assignments are 8, 10, 16, 18, 23, 32, 53, 62, 64, 68, 72.

Starting Talking

The Road Not Taken

Two roads diverged in a yellow wood,
And sorry I could not travel both
And be one traveller, long I stood
And looked down one as far as I could
To where it bent in the undergrowth;

Then took the other, as just as fair,
And having perhaps the better claim,
Because it was grassy and wanted wear;
Though as for that the passing there
Had worn them really about the same,

And both that morning equally lay
In leaves no step had trodden black.
Oh, I kept the first for another day!
Yet knowing how way leads on to way,
I doubted if I should ever come back.

I shall be telling this with a sigh
Somewhere ages and ages hence:
Two roads diverged in a wood, and I —
I took the one less travelled by,
And that has made all the difference.

Robert Frost

Leading in

There are times when sharing ideas about a poem can be helpful. This is an approach which can 'break the ice' when a group starts to explore a poem.

Thinking about the poem

1 Note down any three things that you would like to comment on or ask about. They might be about the whole poem or about bits of it.

2 Form a group of three or four. One of you should read the poem so that everyone in your group can hear it. If you wish, others in the group can read the poem out as well.

3 One member of the group tells the others one of her/his three thoughts or questions. (For example, you might say, 'I don't understand this poem but I get the idea of someone who's lonely.') Working clockwise, each member of the group comments on what has been said so far and tries to add to it – and that can include disagreeing.

4 Now another member of the group should introduce one of his/her three thoughts or questions to the rest of the group. As before, everyone else in turn should add a comment. Repeat this process until everyone in the group has had a chance to start a round of discussion.

5 After everyone has started a round, you can carry on discussing the poem in this formal way or you can discuss it more freely. Whichever you choose, you have the rest of your own list of comments and questions to start from.

If you get stuck at any stage, read the poem again, maybe aloud, to see if it will help you.

Coursework ideas

(*e l*) 1 Write a letter as if to Robert Frost or the writer of another poem in this anthology, telling the poet your views on the poem and the things you would like to ask.

(*e l*) 2 'The Road Not Taken' uses the countryside as its setting. Choose another poem in this anthology which describes a place and uses it to comment on life. Write your commentary on how this poem works for you.

(*e*) 3 Write a poem or story which uses a town or country setting to comment on something in your own life or in the lives of others. This could be one piece of writing in a thematic unit. The choice of theme is up to you, but possibilities include, growing up, being oneself, travelling, decisions.

 **Signposts**

Further poems which lend themselves to this approach are 61, 70, 76, 81.

Poems which could link with coursework assignments are 17, 38, 55, 74.

What's In a Poem?

Purpose: to start exploring a poem through the puzzles and questions it sets going in you and your fellow students.

First Day at School

A millionbillionwillion miles from home
Waiting for the bell to go. (To go where?)
Why are they all so big, other children?
So noisy? So much at home they
must have been born in uniform
Lived all their lives at playgrounds
Spent the years inventing games
that don't let me in. Games
that are rough, that swallow you up.

And the railings.
All round, the railings.
Are they to keep out wolves and monsters?
Things that carry off and eat children?
Things you don't take sweets from?
Perhaps they're to stop us getting out
Running away from the lessins. Lessin.
What does a lessin look like?
Sounds small and slimy.
They keep them in glassrooms.
Whole rooms made out of glass. Imagine.

I wish I could remember my name
Mummy said it would come in useful.
Like wellies. When there's puddles.
Yellowwellies. I wish she was here.
I think my name is sewn on somewhere
perhaps the teacher will read it for me.
Tea-cher. The one who makes the tea.

Roger McGough

Leading in

Some poems are fairly simple. Many are not. They tend to raise questions in your mind and do not always answer them. Here is an approach to help you to go deeper into a poem by sharing and discussing questions that arise as you read and think about it.

Read this poem to yourself to get the general sense and mood of it. It may look and sound simple, almost like a nursery rhyme – but is it?

Thinking about the poem

1 Write down three questions about anything which strikes you in this poem.

They might be about something you genuinely do not understand.

They might be about something to which you think there could be other answers, even though you have one already.

They could be about something you like or do not like, something that you find particularly effective or something that the poem reminds you of. For instance, if you decide that a certain line makes you feel sad, turn that into a question: 'What is it about that line that makes me feel sad?'

2 Share your questions in a small group. Discuss each other's sets of questions and try to answer them. Then decide on the *three* which would be most worthwhile discussing further.

3 From these three, decide as a group on the *main, single question* which you believe it is important for everyone to consider.

4 Before you discuss the poem as a class, make sure that you have read the poem again. Your group can present its main question to the class for further discussion.

Coursework ideas

(*el*) 1 Write an account of what you did. Include the questions you first wrote down; what questions you worked on with the group; which questions were dropped or kept and why; and what made your group choose its final single question.

(*e*) 2 Create a story based on the ideas that you have found and discussed in this poem.

(*e*) 3 Choose another poem and use this 'Asking Questions' approach to help you make notes. Then try to answer your three most important questions in an essay.

 Further poems which lend themselves to this approach are 20, 50, 61.

Poems which could link with coursework assignments are 62, 80.

A Cat

She had a name among the children;
But no one loved though someone owned
Her, locked her out of doors at bedtime
And had her kittens duly drowned.

In Spring, nevertheless, this cat
Ate blackbirds, thrushes, nightingales,
And birds of bright voice and plume and flight,
As well as scraps from neighbours' pails.

I loathed and hated her for this;
One speckle on a thrush's breast
Was worth a million such; and yet
She lived long, till God gave her rest.

Edward Thomas

1 *A Curse on my Former Bank Manager*

May your computer twitch every time it remembers money
until the twitches mount and become a mechanical ache
and may the ache increase until the tapes begin to scream
and may the pus of data burst from its metal skin

and just before the downpour of molten aluminium
may you be preening in front of your computer
and may you be saying to your favourite millionaire
yes it cost nine hundred thousand but it repays every penny

and may the hundred-mile tape which records my debts spring out
like a supersonic two-dimensional boa-constrictor
and may it slip under your faultless collar and surround your hairless neck
and may it tighten and tighten until it has repaid everything I owe you

Adrian Mitchell

2 *Ain't I A Woman?*

That man over there say
    a woman needs to be helped into carriages
and lifted over ditches
    and to have the best place everywhere.
Nobody ever helped me into carriages
    or over mud puddles
        or gives me a best place . . .

And ain't I a woman?
    Look at me
Look at my arm!
    I have plowed and planted
and gathered into barns
    and no man could head me . . .
And ain't I a woman?
    I could work as much
and eat as much as a man –
    when I could get to it –
and bear the lash as well
    and ain't I a woman?
I have born 13 children
    and seen most all sold into slavery
and when I cried out a mother's grief
    none but Jesus heard me . . .

and ain't I a woman?
    that little man in black there say
a woman can't have as much rights as a man
    cause Christ wasn't a woman
Where did your Christ come from?
    From God and a woman!
Man had nothing to do with him!
    If the first woman God ever made
was strong enough to turn the world
    upside down, all alone
together women ought to be able to turn it
    rightside up again.

Sojourner Truth

3 *A Kite Is a Victim*

A kite is a victim you are sure of.
You love it because it pulls
gentle enough to call you master,
strong enough to call you fool;
because it lives
like a desperate trained falcon
in the high sweet air,
and you can always haul it down
to tame it in your drawer.

A kite is a fish you have already caught
in a pool where no fish come,
so you play him carefully and long,
and hope he won't give up,
or the wind die down.

A kite is the last poem you've written,
so you give it to the wind,
but you don't let it go
until someone finds you
something else to do.

A kite is a contract of glory
that must be made with the sun,
so you make friends with the field
the river and the wind,
then you pray the whole cold night before,
under the travelling cordless moon,
to make you worthy and lyric and pure.

Leonard Cohen

4 *Almost Love*

It happen sometimes; a pair of eyes a profile
someone we don't know and see only once
or every afternoon.
Someone we met, it was just like that:
a hand on yours
some hasty words.
But someone who became a part of you
and now there's no seeing that face without paling
without trembling hands
and it's almost love.

Magaly Sánchez

5 *Alsoran*

Your chest hurts twice as bad,
your legs weigh twice as much
when you're alone, adrift
and twenty yards behind the pack.

That special pain that creeps
from chest to shoulder, stabs
beneath the collar bone
and drains all energy away.

Why keep going why keep
thumping on through thick and
thin can't think can't
hardly breathe can't

catch them up can't
keep it up can't
give up now can't face the end
can't win can't stop can't

With easy flowing strides the Blond God
laps you saps
each last despairing flailing
ounce of energy each

Smooth as a tank he glides –
Head Boy next year,
a Scholarship the next and
here, this afternoon, the 1500 metres.

He stands beside the finish being sporting –
the tape sliced,
clean as a whistle,
his from the starting gun:

he's hardly damp. You're sweating like a pig,
wheezing like a broken mattress;
you stagger to a stop,
fall on your knees and puke your dinner up.

With sympathetic smile, he
nimbly skips aside;
you labour on,
his running shoes unsoiled.

Mick Gowar

6 *And Peace Will Come*

and peace will come and the living
men will go
and snow will fall upon the snow
and they will say they
did not die in vain

and another war and another
war will come again
and again and
the living men and the living
men will go and fall
asleep and cover them
with again and snow and
peace will come and all who move
or breathe will come and go

and come and go like leaves and
leaves of centuries of snow
will fall and fall

and peace and war will come
and go and go and come
and cover all and snow
and snow and snow and wind and rain
and snow will fall upon the snow
and peace will come and everyone
will know they did not go in vain

and another sky will die
and come and go again and again
and again
and again
and peace will come

Bernard Kops

7 *Anonymous*

Adieu, the years are a broken song,
And the right grows weak in the strife with wrong,

The lilies of love have a crimson stain
And the old days never will come again.

Anon

From the diary of an Australian soldier,
September 1917

8 *Answers To a Grade-School Biology Test*

To what order do the rats belong?

To a superior order.

Where do they make their homes?

In shelters underground
below the human border.

How are their children born?

    From hydrocarbon links like ours
    but harder.

What do they eat?

    The world's unguarded larder.

Why are they dangerous to human health?

    Because our health is their chief danger.

Have they any use for science?

    For rodent science, yes;
    under the street they think

    and multiply and wait
    till men have cleared themselves
    and cats
    from all the earth that glares at sky
    and there is freedom to preside
    for rats.

                    Earle Birney

9 *As In The Beginning*

A man has two hands and when one
gets caught on the belt and his fingers
are amputated and then patched
he cannot work. His hands are insured
however so he gets some money
for the work his hands have done before.
If he loses a finger he gets a flat sum
of $250 for each digit &/or $100 for a joint
missing for the rest of his stay on earth,
like an empty stool at a beggar's banquet.
When the hands are my father's hands
it makes me cry although my pen must keep scratching
its head across the page of another night.
To you my father is a stranger
and perhaps you think the insurance paid is enough.

Give me my father's hands when they are not broken
and swollen,
give me my father's hands, young again,
and holding the hands of my mother,
give me my father's hands still brown and uncalloused,
beautiful hands that broke bread for us at table,
hands as smooth as marble and naked as the morning,
give me hands without a number tattooed at the wrist,
without the copper sweat of clinging change,
give me my father's hands as they were in the beginning,
whole,
open,
warm
and without fear.

Mary di Michele

10 *Be a Butterfly*

Don't be a kyatta-pilla
Be a butterfly
old preacher screamed
to illustrate his sermon
of Jesus and the higher life

rivulets of well-earned
sweat sliding down
his muscly mahogany face
in the half-empty school church
we sat shaking with muffling
laughter
watching our mother trying to save
herself from joining the wave

only our father remaining poker face
and afterwards we always went home to
split peas Sunday soup
with dumplings, fufu and pigtail

Don't be a kyatta-pilla
Be a butterfly
Be a butterfly

That was de life preacher
and you was right

Grace Nichols

11 Beginnings

In the vast antheap of the world
one little ant thinks differently.

In the snarled traffic of metropolis
a small family car crashes the lights.

Under a tailored and conventional suit
a heart beats out a naked rhythm.

Like a roomsize coloured balloon
a man blows up a religion till it bursts.

Somebody somewhere begins to unpick the stitches
in the bright battle flag of glory.

Gavin Ewart

12 Birds

Your kisses peck me like birds
And lightly scatter like birds, in a wind
Yet their nip and their sweet song
Leave me silent, through storms.

Sue Lenier

13 Blackberry-Picking

For Philip Hobsbaum

Late August, given heavy rain and sun
For a full week, the blackberries would ripen.
At first, just one, a glossy purple clot
Among others, red, green, hard as a knot.
You ate that first one and its flesh was sweet
Like thickened wine: summer's blood was in it
Leaving stains upon the tongue and lust for
Picking. Then red ones inked up and that hunger
Sent us out with milk-cans, pea-tins, jam-pots
Where briars scratched and wet grass bleached our boots.

Round hayfields, cornfields and potato-drills
We trekked and picked until the cans were full,
Until the tinkling bottom had been covered
With green ones, and on top big dark blobs burned
Like a plate of eyes. Our hands were peppered
With thorn pricks, our palms sticky as Bluebeard's.

We hoarded the fresh berries in the byre.
But when the bath was filled we found a fur,
A rat-grey fungus, glutting on our cache.
The juice was stinking too. Once off the bush
The fruit fermented, the sweet flesh would turn sour.
I always felt like crying. It wasn't fair
That all the lovely canfuls smelt of rot.
Each year I hoped they'd keep, knew they would not.

Seamus Heaney

14 *Bye Bye Black Sheep*

Volunteering at seventeen, Uncle Joe
Went to Dunkirk as a Royal Marine
And lived, not to tell the tale.
Demobbed, he brought back a broken 303,
A quiver of bayonets, and a kitbag
Of badges, bullets and swastikas
Which he doled out among warstruck nephews.

With gasflame-blue eyes and dark unruly hair
He could have been God's gift. Gone anywhere.
But a lifetime's excitement had been used up
On his one-and-only trip abroad. Instead,
Did the pools and horses. 'Lash me, I'm bored,'
He'd moan, and use language when Gran
Was out of the room. He was our hero.

But not for long. Apparently he was
No good. Couldn't hold down a job.
Gave the old buck to his Elders and Betters.
Lazy as sin, he turned to drink
And ended up marrying a Protestant.
A regular black sheep was Uncle Joe.
Funny how wrong kids can be.

Roger McGough

15 Cat

The cat within the kitten curled
his way into our lives.
On the first night he crept
under the rusty belly of the fridge
that motored like his mother
but leaked
and flattened out his fur
so that he coughed and shrivelled
almost died
required of us cradling
carrying himself to our hands
with the curving needles of his claws.

Was it just need
that followed us everywhere
falling asleep in our slippers
studying the shape of a shoulder
or the smell of hair?
Soon we awoke to find
his yellow eyes fixed on us,
dragging us back to awareness;
though he was fat and fed
he edged his way into our eating
with his devouring stare.

We are the cat's possessions now.
He allows us to sit on one of the sofas
to eat some vegetarian dishes undisturbed.
He sleeps heavily on our beds.
Rising uncertainly in darkness
I stumble over the swift
and silky ankle-swish
of his self-importance
and I surrender
to this animal absolute
that stakes its claim to survival
and everything else that is there.

Frances Davis

16 *Catalogue*

Cats sleep fat and walk thin.
Cats, when they sleep, slump;
When they wake, stretch and begin
Over, pulling their ribs in.
Cats walk thin.

Cats wait in a lump,
Jump in a streak.
Cats, when they jump, are sleek
As a grape slipping its skin –
They have technique.
Oh, cats don't creak.
They sneak.

Cats sleep fat.
They spread out comfort underneath them
Like a good mat,
As if they picked the place
And then sat;
You walk around one
As if he were the City Hall
After that.

If male,
A cat is apt to sing on a major scale;
This concert is for everybody, this
Is wholesale.
For a baton, he wields a tail.

(He is also found,
When happy, to resound
With an enclosed and private sound.)

A cat condenses.
He pulls in his tail to go under bridges,
And himself to go under fences.
Cats fit
In any size box or kit,
And if a large pumpkin grew under one,
He could arch over it.

When everyone else is just ready to go out,
The cat is just ready to come in.
He's not where he's been.
Cats sleep fat and walk thin.

Rosalie Moore

17 City

What would my Grandma have said
If she could have seen the green
Where once the houses stood,
Last year with red-black brick
And rotten boards and broken glass?

Would she have loved new grass?
Or would she just have moaned
About the loss of foggy yesterday
Where she and Grandad used to play
With whips and spinning tops
Between old cobblestones and chased
Wild arrowed boys back home
Along the narrow alley ways?

John Kitching

18 Counting The Mad

This one was put in a jacket,
This one was sent home,
This one was given bread and meat
But would eat none,
And this one cried No No No No
All day long.

This one looked at the window
As though it were a wall,
This one saw things that were not there,
This one things that were,
And this one cried No No No No
All day long.

This one thought himself a bird,
This one a dog,
And this one thought himself a man,
An ordinary man,
And cried and cried No No No No
All day long.

Donald Justice

19 Cowboy

I remember, on a long
Hot, summer, thirsty afternoon
Hiding behind a rock
With Wyatt Earp
(His glasses fastened on with sellotape)

The Sioux were massing for their last attack

We knew

No 7th Cavalry for us
No bugles blaring in the afternoon
I held my lone star pistol in my hand
Thinking
I was just seven and too young to die
Thinking

Save the last cap
For yourself

Richard Hill

20 Dad

Your old hat hurts me, and those black
　　fat raisins you liked to press into
my palm from your soft heavy hand:
　　I see you staggering back up the path
with sacks of potatoes from some local farm,
　　fresh eggs, flowers. Every day I grieve

for your great heart broken and you gone.
　　You loved to watch the trees. This year
you did not see their Spring.
　　The sky was freezing over the fen
as on that somewhere secretly appointed day
　　you beached: cold, white-faced, shivering.

What happened, old bull, my loyal
　　hoarse-voiced warrior? The hammer
blow that stopped you in your track
　　and brought you to a hospital monitor
could not destroy your courage,
　　to the end you were
uncowed and unconcerned with pleasing anyone.

I think of you now as once again safely
    at my mother's side, the earth as
chosen as a bed, and feel most sorrow for
    all that was gentle in
my childhood buried there
    already forfeit, now for ever lost.

Elaine Feinstein

21 *Daydream*

One day people will touch and talk perhaps easily,
And loving be natural as breathing and warm as sunlight,
And people will untie themselves, as string is unknotted,
Unfold and yawn and stretch and spread their fingers,
Unfurl, uncurl like seaweed returned to the sea,
And work will be simple and swift as a seagull flying,
And play will be casual and quiet as a seagull settling,
And the clocks will stop, and no-one will wonder or
    care or notice,
And people will smile without reason, even in the winter,
    even in the rain.

A.S.J. Tessimond

22 *Dumb Insolence*

I'm big for ten years old
Maybe that's why they get at me

Teachers, parents, cops
Always getting at me

When they get at me

I don't hit em
They can do you for that

I don't swear at em
They can do you for that

I stick my hands in my pockets
And stare at them

And while I stare at them
I think about sick

They call it dumb insolence

They don't like it
But they can't do you for it

I've been done before
They say if I get done again

They'll put me in a home
So I do dumb insolence

Adrian Mitchell

23 *Emperors of the Island*

There is the story of a deserted island
where five men walked down to the bay.

The story of the island is
that three men would two men slay.

Three men dug two graves in the sand,
three men stood on the sea wet rock,
three shadows moved away.

There is the story of a deserted island
where three men walked down to the bay.

The story of this island is
that two men would one man slay.

Two men dug one grave in the sand,
two men stood on the sea wet rock,
two shadows moved away.

There is the story of a deserted island
where two men walked down to the bay.

The story of this island is
that one man would one man slay.

One man dug one grave in the sand,
one man stood on the sea wet rock,
one shadow moved away.

There is the story of a deserted island
where four ghosts walked down to the bay.

The story of this island is
that four ghosts would one man slay.

Four ghosts dug one grave in the sand,
four ghosts stood on the sea wet rock;
five ghosts moved away.

Dannie Abse

24 *Few*

Alone tired halfdrunk hopeful
I staggered into the bogs
at Green Park station
and found 30 written on the wall

Appalled I lurched out
into the windy blaring neon Piccadilly night

thinking surely
Surely there must be more of us than that?

Pete Brown

25 *Fifteen Million Plastic Bags*

I was walking in a government warehouse
Where the daylight never goes.
I saw fifteen million plastic bags
Hanging in a thousand rows.

Five million bags were six feet long
Five million bags were five foot five
Five million were stamped with Mickey Mouse
And they came in a smaller size.

Were they for guns or uniforms
Or a dirty kind of party game?
Then I saw each bag had a number
And every bag bore a name.

And five million bags were six feet long
Five million were five foot five
Five million were stamped with Mickey Mouse
And they came in a smaller size

So I've taken my bag from the hanger
And I've pulled it over my head
And I'll wait for the priest to zip it
So the radiation won't spread

Now five million bags are six feet long
Five million are five foot five
Five million are stamped with Mickey Mouse
And they come in a smaller size.

                                        Adrian Mitchell

26 *God Knows I'm Good*

I was walking through the counters of a national concern
And a cash machine was spitting by my shoulder.
And I saw the multitude of faces, honest, rich and clean
As the merchandise exchanged and money roared.
And a woman hot with worry slyly slipped a tin of stewing steak
into the paper bag at her side.
And her face was white with fear in case her actions were observed
So she closed her eyes to keep her conscience blind.

Crying
    "God knows I'm good,
    God knows I'm good,
    God knows I'm good,
    God may look the other way today.

    God knows I'm good,
    God knows I'm good,
    God knows I'm good,
    God may look the other way today."

Then she moved toward the exit clutching tightly at her paper bag,
Perspiration trickled down her forehead.
And her heart it leapt inside her as the hand laid on her shoulder,
She was led away bewildered and amazed.
Through her deafened ears the cash machines were shrieking on the counter
As her escort asked her softly for her name.
And a crowd of honest people rushed to help a tired old lady
Who had fainted to the whirling wooden floor.

Crying
    "God knows I'm good,
    God knows I'm good,
    God knows I'm good,
    Surely God won't look the other way.

    God knows I'm good,
    God knows I'm good,
    God knows I'm good,
    Surely God won't look the other way."

David Bowie

27 *Haiku*

buckets filled with elder blossom
– such drunkenness between us
shredding petals for wine

two extra in our household –
a butterfly
        clings to the green curtain
he stays for winter only
the new child
        a guest for many seasons

Frances Horovitz

28 *Hero*

"Of course I took the drugs. Look, son,
there's no fair play, no gentlemen,
no amateurs, just winning.
How old are you? Fifteen? Well,
you should know that
no one runs for fun – well, not beyond
the schoolboy stuff – eleven or twelve years old.
I'd been a pro for years;
my job – to get that Gold.

Mind you, we English are an odd lot:
like to believe we love the slob that fails,
the gentlemanly third; so any gap-toothed yob who gets the glory
also gets some gentlemanly trait: helps cripples get across
the street, nice to small animals. You know the kind of thing,
it helps the public feel it's
all legit; that sportsmanship is real and that
it's all clean fun –
the strongest, bravest, fittest
best man won.

Yeah, Steroids . . . Who do *you* think? . . . Oh, don't be wet –
My coach, of course, he used to get them
through this vet . . . The side effects? Well, not so bad
as these things go – for eighteen months or so
I didn't have much use for girls. But, by then I was training
for the Big One – got to keep the body pure,
not waste an ounce of effort."

He gives a great guffaw.
A chain of spittle
rattles down the front of
his pyjama jacket.
He wipes his mouth;
His eyes don't laugh at all.

". . . Do it again? Of course I would –
I'd cheat, I'd box, I'd spike, I'd pay the devil's price
to be that good again
for just one day. You see, at twenty-three
I peaked – got all I ever wanted:
all anyone would ever want from me.
After the race, this interviewer told me
Fifty million people's hopes and dreams had been
fulfilled – a Gold!
How many ever get that chance? I did.
Would you say No to that?
Of course not.

Damn, the bell. You'd better go, they're pretty strict.
Yeah, leave the flowers there on the top,
the nurse'll get some water and a vase."

Mick Gowar

29 Hot Summer Sunday

Especially on hot summer Sundays
my Grandpa liked to rest
supine in the narrow bathtub
soaking in curved cool water
sometimes flipping his toes
or, quite child-like,
toying with a pale green soapcake,
but mostly
staying motionless, eyes closed,
lips half-smiling,
limbs outstretched.

That hot summer Sunday
when I looked at him
straightly lying, lips parted,
silent in the shallow trough,
a foam of white, frothed and lacy,
set as new suds
about his shaven jawbones,
it seemed he might stir,
whistle a relaxed sigh,
unclose those eyelids,
ask me to scrub his back.

A.L. Hendricks

30 How Do I Love Thee?

How do I love thee? Let me count the ways.
I love thee to the depth and breadth and height
My soul can reach, when feeling out of sight
For the ends of Being and Ideal Grace.
I love thee to the level of every day's
Most quiet need, by sun and candlelight.
I love thee freely, as men strive for Right;
I love thee purely, as they turn from Praise;
I love thee with the passion put to use
In my old griefs, and with my childhood's faith;
I love thee with a love I seemed to lose
With my lost saints, – I love thee with the breath,
Smiles, tears, of all my life! – and, if God choose,
I shall but love thee better after death.

Elizabeth Barrett Browning

31 *In-a Brixtan Markit*

I walk in-a Brixtan markit,
believin I a respectable man,
you know. An wha happn?

Policeman come straight up
an search mi bag!
Man – straight to mi.
Like them did a-wait fi mi.
Come search mi bag, man.

Fi mi bag!
An wha them si in deh?
Two piece a yam, a dasheen,
a han a banana, a piece a pork
an mi lates Bob Marley.

Man all a suddn I feel
mi head nah fi mi. This yah now
is when man kill somody, nah!

'Tony', I sey, 'hol on. Hol on,
Tony. Dohn shove. Dohn shove.
Dohn move neidda fis, tongue
nor emotion. Battn down, Tony.
Battn down.' An, man, Tony win.

James Berry

32 *'In This City . . .'*

In this city, perhaps a street.
In this street, perhaps a house.
In this house, perhaps a room
And in this room a woman sitting,
Sitting in the darkness, sitting and crying
For someone who has just gone through the door
And who has just switched off the light
Forgetting she was there.

Alan Brownjohn

33 'It Will Not Change'

It will not change now
    After so many years;
Life has not broken it
    With parting or tears;
Death will not alter it,
    It will live on
In all my songs for you
    When I am gone.

Sarah Teasdale

34 Kite

I took a kite, not mine, up
To the edge of the town. High
It jerked, bounding
Against the tether which I clung to, knowing
A second's lessening of panic would lose it to me.

Then it steadied, and as it lay on the air
The breath came back into my body. Up there
It floated, and lifted as I turned my wrist.
I felt my movement held the kite to me.

It steadied and my mind moved
Safe once up there
In that blue circle, held within its edge,
Riding at anchor, calm as the kite's riding,
On top of the tugging now, holding the world.

The kite seems mine now, but –
The cord snatched through my palm and
Oh, here I go, up into it and
Help, now I can't let go, won't because –
        But oh,
Where is the safe sphere I was gazing at
That one blue?
That place complete to the view
Is now the air I breathe
Gulping I cannot see it.
Countless slivers of light beat round my eyes,

And the eye of the kite, staring above, not helping.

Jenny Joseph

35 Looking For Nancy

Looking for Nancy
     everywhere, I've stopped
girls in trenchcoats
and blue dresses,
     said
Nancy, I've looked
     all over
     hell for you,
Nancy I've been afraid
I'd die before I found you.

     But there's always
     been some mistake:

a broken streetlight,
too much rum
     or even
my wanting too much
for it to be her.

Alden Nowlan

36 Mastering the Craft

To make the big time you must learn
The basic moves: left jab and hook,
The fast one-two, right-cross; the block
And counter-punch; the way to turn
Opponents on the ropes; the feint
To head or body; uppercut;
To move inside the swing and set
Your man up for the kill. But don't
Think that this is all; a mere
Beginning only. It is through
Fighting often you will grow
Accomplished in manoeuvres more
Subtle than the textbooks know:
How to change your style to meet
The unexpected move that might
Leave you open to the blow
That puts the lights out for the night.

The same with poets: they must train,
Practise metre's footwork, learn
The old iambic left and right,
To change the pace and how to hold
The big punch till the proper time,
Jab away with accurate rhyme;
Adapt the style or be knocked cold.
But first the groundwork must be done.
Those poets who have never learnt
The first moves of the game, they can't
Hope to win.
      Yet here comes one,
No style, at all, untrained and fat,
Who still contrives to knock you flat.

Vernon Scannell

37 *Message*

In the corner
where the sun never shines
I will wait for you.

And if you come,
I will greet you softly
and hold your hands in mine.

The corner is cold, however,
and the dust gathers there.
The wind whirls it around.

I will not wait too long.
There are others to see,
they will be kind to me.

Jim Burns

38 Moment

Two children emerge from a wood,
laughing as they come
swimming last year's leaves;
flowers in their hands.
They hold each other close,
until the sun strikes grass,
they dance and shout and sing
and tumble down the fields.
They call and wave and wave at me
where I gaze through glass.
If I don't look the other way,
they'll fall into my eyes.
With snowdrops they have come to stay;
I drink them on the train.

Bernard Kops

39 Move On

They made love under bridges, lacking beds,
And engines whistled them a bridal song,
A sudden bull's-eye showed them touching heads,
Policemen told them they were doing wrong;
And when they slept on seats in public gardens
Told them, 'Commit no nuisance in the park';
The beggars, begging the policemen's pardons,
Said that they thought as it was after dark –

At this the law grew angry and declared
Outlaws who outrage by-laws are the devil;
At this the lovers only stood and stared,
As well they might, for they had meant no evil;
'Move on,' the law said. To avoid a scene
They moved. And thus we keep our cities clean.

William Plomer

40 *Mr and Mrs*

Mr and Mrs in matching tracksuits
on an evening out at the megastore,
with matching tracksuited children
needing nothing wanting more

new company car every August
an extra 5 mph and the latest reg,
whatever she puts in the microwave
always comes out meat and two veg.

His and Hers towelling bathrobes
initials on everything they own,
even the cat and the children
Mantovani on the answerphone

his ambition's to join the masons
hers is to be on TV,
they'll have anything that's expensive
and anything that's absolutely free.

Mr and Mrs Upwardly Mobile
trying to find their place,
in the sun then rise above it
staying ahead in the human race

remembering where they've come from
imagining where they're bound,
from a dot on the map Dad in cloth cap
to a 5-bed detached in own grounds.

The sons and daughters of Labour,
fathers and mothers of Thatcherism
body-builders/head-shrinkers
the new ruling class of Great Britain

less labour aristocracy
than lumpen bourgeoisie,
rich white trash
on a lifelong spending spree.

Andy Pearmain

41 *Mrs Swipe Speaks Out*

So I said to her I said
I'm not one to complain
I said as you know only too well
I said but if you think I'm going to
put up with this nonsense indefinitely
you've got another think coming oh yes I said
please don't think you can come the bounce
on me I said because I've had just about
enough thank you very much I said
you can walk the whole length and breadth
of Varicose Street I said and you won't find
a more long-suffering and charitable
person than yours truly I said
but like the Good Book says every worm
must have its day and mine is
just around the corner I said so you needn't
stand there looking four-eyed and fish-faced
as if Meadow-Lea wouldn't melt in your mouth
since I have not the slightest intention of
prolonging this conversation any further
live and let live I said even though it seems
to me there's some as would be hard-pressed
to justify their miserable
existence naming no names of course
and I dropped the paper parcel of prawn-shells
over her side of the fence I believe
these are yours madam I said and although
it was a horrible cold day the look on its face
as I walked away kept me warm as toast
for the rest of the morning!

Bruce Dawe

42 *My Father's Hands*

My father's hands
are beautiful, they can
fix this moth's wing and make
machines
they can mend the fuse when the world
goes dark
can make light swim and walls jump
in around me again
I can see my mother's face again.

You must take good care of them with
your finest creams
never let the nails break or
skin go dry, only those wise fingers
know how to fix the thing
that makes my doll cry and they make
small animals out of clay.

Never let blades or anything sharp
and hurtful near them
don't let bees or nettles
sting them don't let fire or burning oil
try them

My father's hands are beautiful, take
good care of them

Jeni Couzyns

43 *My Kid Brother*

Not picked for chain-he,
squatting on the low wall
two bricks high
around the flower bed
around the tree,
scuffing the loose gravel:
builds a pile between his feet

Mutters to himself as though absorbed
picks
at the moss
between the bricks
between his knees
pick pick pick don't look
pick pick pick don't look up

A lone ant crawls too near,
he crunches it;
throws back his head –
Punched by the flashbulb sun
the water floods his eyes
but still his hands attack
the moss
head down he clears
a . . . drainage ditch?
between the bricks

with total
concentration. No-
one asks the question,
            'What you doing?'

Anyone can see
he didn't want to play
that game:
got plenty better things
to do

pick
pick pick
pick pick pick

                    Mick Gowar

44 *Nature Table*

The tadpoles won't keep still in the aquarium;
Ben's tried seven times to count them –
thirty-two, thirty-three, wriggle, wriggle –
all right, he's got better things to do.

Heidi stares into the tank, wearing
a snail on her knuckle like a ring.
She can see purple clouds in the water,
a sky for the tadpoles in their world.

Matthew's drawing a worm. Yesterday
he put one down Elizabeth's neck.
But these are safely locked in the wormery
eating their mud; he's tried that too.

Laura sways with her nose in a daffodil,
drunk on pollen, her eyes tight shut.
The whole inside of her head is filling
with a slow hum of fizzy yellow.

Tom squashes his nose against the window.
He hopes it may look like a snail's belly
to the thrush outside. But is not attacked:
the thrush is happy on the bird-table.

The wind ruffles a chaffinch's crest
and gives the sparrows frilly grey knickers
as they squabble over their seeds and bread.
The sun swings in and out of clouds.

Ben's constructing a wigwam of leaves
for the snails. Heidi whispers to the tadpoles
'Promise you won't start eating each other!'
Matthew's rather hoping they will.

A wash of sun sluices the window,
bleaches Tom's hair blonder, separates
Laura from her daffodil with a sneeze,
and sends the tadpoles briefly frantic;

until the clouds flop down again
grey as wet canvas. The wind quickens,
birds go flying, window-glass rattles,
pellets of hail are among the birdseed.

Fleur Adcock

45 *Nooligan*

I'm a nooligan
dont give a toss
in our class
I'm the boss
(well, one of them)

I'm a nooligan
got a nard 'ead
step out of line
and youre dead
(well, bleedin)

I'm a nooligan
I spray me name
all over town
footballs me game
(well, watchin)

I'm a nooligan
violence is fun
gonna be a nassassin
or a nired gun
(well, a soldier)

Roger McGough

46 *O My Luve's like a Red, Red Rose*

O my Luve's like a red, red rose
　　That's newly sprung in June:
O my Luve's like the melodie
　　That's sweetly play'd in tune.

As fair art thou, my bonnie lass,
　　So deep in luve am I:
And I will luve thee still, my dear,
　　Till a' the seas gang dry:

Till a' the seas gang dry, my dear,
　　And the rocks melt wi' the sun;
I will luve thee still, my dear,
　　While the sands o' life shall run.

And fare thee weel, my only Luve!
　　And fare thee weel a while!
And I will come again, my Luve,
　　Tho' it were ten thousand mile.

Robert Burns

47 *One Perfect Rose*

A single flow'r he sent me, since we met.
　　All tenderly his messenger he chose;
Deep-hearted, pure, with scented dew still wet –
　　One perfect rose.

I knew the language of the floweret;
　　"My fragile leaves," it said, "his heart enclose."
Love long has taken for his amulet
　　One perfect rose.

Why is it no one ever sent me yet
　　One perfect limousine, do you suppose?
Ah no, it's always just my luck to get
　　One perfect rose.

Dorothy Parker

48 Photographs of Pioneer Women

You can see from their faces
Life was not funny,
The streets, when there were streets,
Tugging at axles,
The settlement ramshackle as a stack of cards.
And where there were no streets, and no houses,
Save their own roof of calico or thatch,
The cows coming morning and afternoon
From the end-of-world swamp,
Udders cemented with mud.

There is nothing to equal pioneering labour
For wrenching a woman out of shape,
Like an old willow, uprooted, thickening.
See their strong arms, their shoulders broadened
By the rhythmical swing of the axe, or humped
Under loads they donkeyed on their backs.
Some of them found time to be photographed,
With bearded husband, and twelve or thirteen children,
Looking shocked, but relentless,
After first starching the frills in their caps.

Ruth Dallas

49 Pigeons

They paddle with staccato feet
in powder-pools of sunlight,
small blue busybodies
strutting like fat gentlemen
with hands clasped
under their swallowtail coats;
and as they stump about,
their heads like tiny hammers
tap at imaginary nails
in non-existent walls.

Elusive ghosts of sunshine
slither down the green gloss
of their necks an instant, and are gone.

Summer hangs drugged from sky to earth
in limpid fathoms of silence:
only warm dark dimples of sound
slide like slow bubbles
from the contented throats.

Raise a casual hand –
with one quick gust
they fountain into air.

                              Richard Kell

50 *Pigeons at the Oppenheimer Park*

I wonder why these pigeons in the Oppenheimer Park
are never arrested and prosecuted for trespassing
on private property and charged with public indecency.

Every day I see these insolent birds perched
on "Whites Only" benches, defying all authority.
Don't they know of the Separate Amenities Act?
A white policeman in full uniform, complete
with a holstered .38 special, passes by
without even raising a reprimanding finger
at offenders who are flouting the law.
They not only sit on the hallowed benches,
they also mess them up with birdshit.

Oh! Holy Ideology! look at those two at the crest
of the jumping impala, they are making love in full
view of madams, hobos, giggling office girls.
What is the world coming to?
Where's the sacred Immorality Act? Sies!

                              Oswald Mashali

51 Poem (For Diz, Who Is 17)

One night we talked of what we loved
Outside ourselves.
Crumpled together on a dark suburban platform,
Our lips were streaked with rain.
The bones of your face polished cold by the wind,
The breath of your voice warm and wet and clear.
    You said that you loved dancing to wild music;
(I, with solemn information, spoke on modern jazz, its
polyrhythmic innovations . . .)
    You loved brightness in pictures;
(I spoke at length, as usual, on Salvador Dali,
displaying knowledge . . .)
    You loved books that you felt for;
(I spoke with gravity on Lawrence Durrell, his significance,
and so forth . . .)
    Suddenly your lips shone in delight, your eyes spun round with pleasure,
    Your voice leapt off-key in its defiant joy:
'Most of all, I love children; and love-making.'
I could only stare into the dark,
Ashamed.

Paul Green

52 Police Beat

When a man is overcome by the police
there is always a moment
when he looks as bewildered
as you or I would
if we woke up out in the street
without the faintest idea
of how we'd got there
and were suddenly handcuffed.
    Soon it comes back to him
and he pulls himself together
and looks scared or cocky
as they hustle him into the car.
    But there's always that moment
when even the toughest of them
looks as if he were struggling to remember.

Alden Nowlan

53   *Scrawny's Surefire Acne Cure*

The thing with acne is your parents
who think it's some modern invention
caused by cokes and chocolate bars.
Truth is it's probably as old as sex.
Think of it. Helen of Troy stayin in
with a big zit on her perfect nose,
Cleopatra before a date rubbin sand
on her cheeks to grind the pimples off,
Lancelot shinin up his best shield
so he can pop a coupala white-tops.
It kinda helps to think all those
heroes went through the same thing.
Okay so I'm crazy but I could be rich
with acne clinics all across Canada
cause I developed a surefire treatment,
scarless, painless and inexpensive.
First apply a cloth dipped in hot water.
The heat draws the gunk to a head
and sterilizes the whole operation.
Then when you got it ready to pop
press a strip of adhesive tape on it
and give it some time and more heat
so it merges real good with the tape,
then rip off the tape fast and, look ma
no pimple – it's stuck onto the tape
and you've just got this little hole
which you dab with another hot cloth.
Well, now you got my secret method
Scrawny's genuine "Zap your Zit Kit"
and I'm not any the richer for it.
Of course, your folks will still nag
about the cokes and chocolate bars
but Lancelot probably had that too.

Gary Hyland

54 *Search and Destroy*

A Bi-Centenary Poem

Fear no more the heat o' the sun
— its rays are filtered, every one.

The fumes from car-exhausts and fires
from dumps and furnaces aspires

to poison heaven where the bird
sings on a diminished third

or totters from the well-sprayed tree
replete with years and DDT.

Now nature grinds her basic gears,
the big-end knocks, the junk-yard nears . . .

Now fish float belly-up downstream caught
by chemicals too vague to be fought,

the forests sigh and fall, the hills
blink badly as the new wind chills,

the grasslands waver and are gone,
the concrete Nothing blunders on,

black gold fountains to the sky,
the sands are mined, the sea-coasts die,

the land runs ruin to our pride!
Lord, give us, for our patricide,

two hundred more years like the last
and what shall then withstand the blast?

Bruce Dawe

55 Soil

A field with tall hedges and a young
Moon in the branches and one star
Declining westward set the scene
Where he works slowly astride the rows
Of red mangolds and green swedes
Plying mechanically his cold blade.

This is his world, the hedge defines
The mind's limits; only the sky
Is boundless, and he never looks up;
His gaze is deep in the dark soil,
As are his feet. The soil is all;
His hands fondle it, and his bones
Are formed out of it with the swedes.
And if sometimes the knife errs,
Burying itself in his shocked flesh,
Then out of the wound the blood seeps home
To the warm soil from which it came.

R.S. Thomas

56 The Snow

In no way that I chose to go
Could I escape the falling snow.

I shut my eyes, wet with my fears:
The snow still whispered at my ears.

I stopped my ears in deaf disguise:
The snow still fell before my eyes.

Snow was my comrade, snow my fate,
In a country huge and desolate.

My footsteps made a shallow space,
And then the snow filled up the place,

And all the walking I had done
Was on a journey not begun.

I did not know the distance gone,
But resolutely travelled on

While silently on every hand
Fell the sorrow of the land,

And no way that I chose to go
Could lead me from the grief of snow.

Clifford Dyment

57 *Sounds of the Day*

When a clatter came,
it was horses crossing the ford.
When the air creaked, it was
a lapwing seeing us off the premises
of its private marsh. A snuffling puff
ten yards from the boat was the tide blocking and
unblocking a hole in a rock.
When the black drums rolled, it was water
falling sixty feet into itself.

When the door
scraped shut, it was the end
of all the sounds there are.

You left me
beside the quietest fire in the world.

I thought I was hurt in my pride only,
forgetting that,
when you plunge your hand in freezing water,
you feel
a bangle of ice round your wrist
before the whole hand goes numb.

Norman MacCaig

58 *Spiders*

Why does she like spiders?
Bitty as beads, fat as comfits,
Treading the air in kitchen and bathroom,
Shinning up pipes to strand themselves
In porcelain wastelands:
What's the attraction?

She argues: they have personality.
I wouldn't know,
I've never talked to one.
Each autumn they invade my house,
Cramming their eggs in corners,
Cosy as cotton-wool inside an ear.

They pay their way. Each window
Is a boneyard. What I resent
(Not on behalf of flies)
Is their stupidity. They drown
In puddles, roast in burning logs:
It's carelessness, not suicide.

And yet she grieves.
These juicy yo-yos, mithering their young
Are all her creatures.
Cats may not kill them,
Birds are given crumbs.
Careful, she says, here comes a big one.

Philip Oakes

59 *Strawberries*

There were never strawberries
like the ones we had
that sultry afternoon
sitting on the step
of the open french window
facing each other
your knees held in mine
the blue plates in our laps
the strawberries glistening
in the hot sunlight
we dipped them in sugar
looking at each other
not hurrying the feast
for one to come
the empty plates
laid on the stone together
with the two forks crossed
and I bent towards you
sweet in that air
in my arms
abandoned like a child
from your eager mouth
the taste of strawberries
in my memory
lean back again
let me love you
let the sun beat
on our forgetfulness
one hour of all
the heat intense
and summer lightning
on the Kilpatrick hills

let the storm wash the plates

Edwin Morgan

60 *The Battle*

Helmet and rifle, pack and overcoat
Marched through a forest. Somewhere up ahead
Guns thudded. Like the circle of a throat
The night on every side was turning red.

They halted and they dug. They sank like moles
Into the clammy earth between the trees.
And soon the sentries, standing in their holes,
Felt the first snow. Their feet began to freeze.

At dawn the first shell landed with a crack.
Then shells and bullets swept the icy woods.
This lasted many days. The snow was black.
The corpses stiffened in their scarlet hoods.

Most clearly of that battle I remember
The tiredness in eyes, how hands looked thin
Around a cigarette, and the bright ember
Would pulse with all the life there was within.

Louis Simpson

61 *The Child Who Walks Backwards*

My next-door neighbour tells me
her child runs into things.
Cupboard corners and doorknobs
have pounded their shapes
into his face. She says
he is bothered by dreams,
rises in sleep from his bed
to steal through the halls
and plummet like a wounded bird
down the flight of stairs.

This child who climbed my maple
with the sureness of a cat
trips in his room, cracks
his skull on the bedpost,
smacks his cheeks on the floor.
When I ask about the burns
on the back of his knee,
his mother tells me
he walks backwards
into fireplace grates
or sits and stares at flames
while sparks burn stars in his skin.

Other children write their names
on the casts that hold
his small bones.
His mother tells me
he runs into things,
walks backwards,
breaks his leg
while she lies
sleeping.

Lorna Crozier

62 *The Execution*

On the night of the execution
a man at the door
mistook me for the coroner.
"Press," I said.

But he didn't understand. He led me
into the wrong room
where the sheriff greeted me:
"You're late, Padre."

"You're wrong," I told him. "I'm Press."
"Yes, of course, Reverend Press."
We went down a stairway.

"Ah, Mr. Ellis," said the Deputy.
"Press!" I shouted. But he shoved me
through a black curtain.
The lights were so bright
I couldn't see the faces
of the men sitting
opposite. But, thank God, I thought
they can see me!

"Look!" I cried. "Look at my face!
Doesn't anybody know me?"

Then a hood covered my head.
"Don't make it harder for us," the hangman whispered.

Alden Nowlan

63 *The Face Of Hunger*

I counted ribs on his concertina chest:
bones protruding as if chiselled
by a sculptor's hand of Famine.

He looked with glazed pupils
seeing only a bun on some sky high shelf.

The skin was pale and taut
like a glove on a doctor's hand.

His tongue darted in and out
like a chameleon's
snatching a confetti of flies.

O! child,
your stomach is a den of lions
roaring day and night.

Oswald Mashali

64   *The Jungle Husband*

Dearest Evelyn, I often think of you
Out with the guns in the jungle stew
Yesterday I hittapotamus
I put the measurements down for you but they got lost in the fuss
It's not a good thing to drink out here
You know, I've practically given it up dear.
Tomorrow I am going alone a long way
Into the jungle. It is all gray
But green on top
Only sometimes when a tree has fallen
The sun comes down plop, it is quite appalling.
You never want to go in a jungle pool
In the hot sun, it would be the act of a fool
Because it's always full of anacondas, Evelyn, not looking ill-fed
I'll say. So no more now, from your loving husband, Wilfred.

Stevie Smith

65   *The Lesson*

Then Jesus took his disciples up the mountain
and gathering them around him he taught them
saying
blessed are the poor in spirit for theirs is the kingdom of heaven
blessed are the meek
blessed are they that mourn
blessed are the merciful
blessed are they who thirst for justice
blessed are all the concerned
blessed are you when persecuted
blessed are you when you suffer
be glad and rejoice for your reward is great in heaven
try to remember what I'm telling you

Then Simon Peter said
      will this count?
and Andrew said
      will we have a test on it?
and James said
      when do we have to know it for?
and Phillip said
      how many words?
and Bartholemew said
      will I have to stand up in front of the others?
and John said
      the other disciples didn't have to learn this
and Matthew said
      how many marks do we get for it?
and Judas said
      what is it worth?
and the other disciples likewise.

Then one of the Pharisees who was present
asked to see Jesus' lesson plan
and inquired of Jesus
his terminal objectives in the cognitive domain

and Jesus wept.

Don Linehan

66 *The Little Cart*

The little cart jolting and banging through the yellow haze of dusk.
   The man pushing behind: the woman pulling in front.
They have left the city and do not know where to go.
"Green, green, those elm-leaves; *they* will cure my hunger,
If only we could find some quiet place and sup on them together."

   The wind has flattened the yellow mother-wort:
   Above it in the distance they see the walls of a house.
"*There* surely must be people living who'll give you something to eat."
They tap at the door, but no one comes: they look in, but the kitchen is empty.
They stand hesitating in the lonely road and their tears fall like rain.

Chen Tzü-Lung

67 *The Little Shoes that Died*

These are the little shoes that died.
    We could not keep her still,
But all day long her busy feet
    Danced to her eager will.

Leaving the body's loving warmth,
    The spirit ran outside;
Then from the shoes they slipped her feet,
    And the little shoes died.

Mary Gilmore

68 *'There Are So Many Tictoc'*

there are so many tictoc
clocks everywhere telling people
what tactic time it is for
tictic instance five toc minutes toc
past six tic

Spring is not regulated and does
not get out of order nor do
its hands a little jerking move
over numbers slowly

        we do not
wind it up it has no weights
springs wheels inside of
its slender self no indeed dear
nothing of the kind.

(So, when kiss Spring comes
we'll kiss each kiss other on kiss the kiss
lips because tic clocks toc don't make
a toctic difference
to kisskiss you and to
kiss me)

e.e. cummings

69 'There Will Come Soft Rains'

War Time

There will come soft rains and the smell of the ground,
And swallows circling with their shimmering sound;

And frogs in the pools singing at night,
And wild plum-trees in tremulous white;

Robins will wear their feathery fire
Whistling their whims on a low fence-wire;

And not one will know of the war, not one
Will care at last when it is done.

Not one would mind, neither bird nor tree,
If mankind perished utterly;

And Spring herself, when she woke at dawn,
Would scarcely know that we were gone.

                                        Sarah Teasdale

70 The Secret in the Cat

I took my cat apart
to see what made him purr.
Like an electric clock
or like the snore

of a warming kettle,
something fizzled and sizzled in him.
Was he a soft car,
the engine bubbling sound?

Was there a wire beneath his fur,
or humming throttle?
I undid his throat.
Within was no stir.

I opened up his chest
as though it were a door:
no whisk or rattle there.
I lifted off his skull:

no hiss or murmur.
I halved his little belly
but found no gear,
no cause for static.

So I replaced his lid,
laced his little gut.
His heart into his vest I slid
and buttoned up his throat.

His tail rose to a rod
and beckoned to the air.
Some voltage made him vibrate
warmer than before.

Whiskers and a tail:
perhaps they caught
some radar code
emitted as a pip, a dot-and-dash

of woollen sound.
My cat a kind of tuning fork? –
amplifier? – telegraph? –
doing secret signal work?

His eyes elliptic tubes:
there's a message in his stare.
I stroke him
but cannot find the dial.

                    May Swenson

71 *The Thickness of Ice*

At first we will meet as friends
(Though secretly I'll be hoping
We'll become much more
And hoping that you're hoping that too).

At first we'll be like skaters
Testing the thickness of ice
(With each meeting
We'll skate nearer the centre of the lake).

Later we will become less anxious to impress,
Less eager than the skater going for gold,
(The triple jumps and spins
Will become an old routine:
We will be content with simple movements).

Later we will not notice the steady thaw,
The creeping cracks will be ignored,
(And one day when the ice gives way
We will scramble to save ourselves
And not each other).

Last of all we'll meet as acquaintances
(Though secretly we will be enemies,
Hurt by missing out on a medal,
Jealous of new partners).

Last of all we'll be like children
Having learnt the thinness of ice,
(Though secretly, perhaps, we may be hoping
To break the ice between us
And maybe meet again as friends).

Liz Loxley

72 *The Wanderer*

Twas the voice of the Wanderer, I heard her exclaim,
You have weaned me too soon, you must nurse me again,
She taps as she passes at each window pane,
Pray, does she not know that she taps in vain?

Her voice flies away on the midnight wind,
But would she be happier if she were within?
She is happier far where the night winds fall,
And there are no doors and no windows at all.

No man has seen her, this pitiful ghost,
And no woman either, but heard her at most,
Sighing and tapping and sighing again,
You have weaned me too soon, you must nurse me again.

Stevie Smith

73 *The Way through the Woods*

They shut the road through the woods
Seventy years ago.
Weather and rain have undone it again,
And now you would never know
There was once a road through the woods
Before they planted the trees.
It is underneath the coppice and heath
And the thin anemones.
Only the keeper sees
That, where the ring-dove broods,
And the badgers roll at ease,
There was once a road through the woods.

Yet, if you enter the woods
Of a summer evening late,
When the night-air cools on the trout-ringed pools
Where the otter whistles his mate,
(They fear not men in the woods,
Because they see so few.)
You will hear the beat of a horse's feet,
And the swish of a skirt in the dew,
Steadily cantering through
The misty solitudes,

As though they perfectly knew
The old lost road through the woods. . . .
But there is no road through the woods.

Rudyard Kipling

74 *The Wilderness*

This is the wilderness my uncle said:
A corner of the garden he'd let go,
Grass waist high and trees grown spindly
Because they were too close together,
A contrast to the rose beds, well mown lawn
And ranks of vegetables. There we would play
Where Indians, outlaws and rugged pioneers
Haunted that patch of wonder surviving
In a suburb. It's all gone now: childhood, uncle,
The patch sold to more determined gardeners.
To remember is to miss that place
Where imagination grew, lost now
In the cautious cultivation of our days.
'All gardens should have one,' uncle said,
We should have listened to him.

John Cotton

75 *The Woman In The Bread Shop*

She guards the counter
in her nylon checks,
lips tight as a barnacle,
'No doughnuts,' she lies,
drilling her eyes through my shopping bag.
'Just a small wholemeal then';
my eyes indicating that I have seen the small wholemeals.
A bundle of TNT is slid cautiously
over the counter
in the guise of a tissue-clad loaf.
'That it?'
She pouts her blue overalled bust at me
and rings the till like a rifle shot.

Ros Barber

76 *Videodrone*

They're falling about with laughter
So much so that everyone in the pub
Is looking over at our table.
Me, I remain untouched, unmoved
As you recount yet another scene
From the latest video you've seen.
As the hilarity subsides
You wipe the froth from your mouth
And reassure us (and yourself) that
'I only watch them for a laugh.'
Ha ha ha
And as you launch into lyrical lewdity
I try and picture the real scene
Of you at home with the video machine.
Curtains drawn, lights so dim,
Carlsberg, Kleenex and carnal sin.
I picture your face
As the fourth hero slams it in,
And that isn't a smile I can see
It is a look of envy.
Do you wish that you were there?
And, correct me if I'm wrong,
But I didn't hear you laugh
As he held her head down in the bath.
There's a deadness in your eyes
Not a happy grin
As the blood flows out
And the drill goes in.
Ha ha ha
Again, everyone looks over,
And the laughter is infectious.
Oh, you're the life and soul
The life and the soul.

The truth is
I should feel sorry for you
But I don't because
You should feel ashamed of yourself
And you don't.
Then again, you only watch them for a laugh,
Don't you?

                              Mark Roberts

77 *Waiting*

My love will come
will fling open her arms and fold me in them,
will understand my fears, observe my changes.
In from the pouring dark, from the pitch night
without stopping to bang the taxi door
she'll run upstairs through the decaying porch
burning with love and love's happiness,
she'll run dripping upstairs, she won't knock,
will take my head in her hands,
and when she drops her overcoat on a chair,
it will slide to the floor in a blue heap.

Yevgeni Yevtushenko

78 *We Are Going*

For Grannie Coolwell

They came in to the little town
A semi-naked band subdued and silent,
All that remained of their tribe.
They came here to the place of their old bora ground
Where now the many white men hurry about like ants.
Notice of estate agent reads: 'Rubbish May Be Tipped Here'.
Now it half covers the traces of the old bora ring.
They sit and are confused, they cannot say their thoughts:
'We are as strangers here now, but the white tribe are the strangers.
We belong here, we are of the old ways.
We are the corroboree and the bora ground,
We are the old sacred ceremonies, the laws of the elders.
We are the wonder tales of Dream Time, the tribal legends told.
We are the past, the hunts and the laughing games, the wandering camp fires.
We are the lightning-bolt over Gaphembah Hill
Quick and terrible,
And the Thunderer after him, that loud fellow.
We are the quiet daybreak paling the dark lagoon.
We are the shadow-ghosts creeping back as the camp fires burn low,
We are nature and the past, all the old ways
Gone now and scattered.
The scrubs are gone, the hunting and the laughter.
The eagle is gone, the emu and the kangaroo are gone from this place.
The bora ring is gone.
The corroboree is gone.
And we are going.'

Kath Walker

79 'We Are Going to See The Rabbit...'

We are going to see the rabbit,
We are going to see the rabbit.
Which rabbit, people say?
Which rabbit, ask the children?
Which rabbit?
The only rabbit,
The only rabbit in England,
Sitting behind a barbed-wire fence
Under the floodlights, neon lights,
Sodium lights,
Nibbling grass
On the only patch of grass
In England, in England
(Except the grass by the hoardings
Which doesn't count.)
We are going to see the rabbit
And we must be there on time.

First we shall go by escalator,
Then we shall go by underground,
And then we shall go by motorway
And then by helicopterway,
And the last ten yards we shall have to go
On foot.

And now we are going
All the way to see the rabbit,
We are nearly there,
We are longing to see it,
And so is the crowd
Which is here in thousands
With mounted policemen
And big loudspeakers
And bands and banners,
And everyone has come a long way.

But soon we shall see it
Sitting and nibbling
The blades of grass
On the only patch of grass
In – but something has gone wrong!
Why is everyone so angry,
Why is everyone jostling
And slanging and complaining?

The rabbit has gone,
Yes, the rabbit has gone.
He has actually burrowed down into the earth
And made himself a warren, under the earth,
Despite all these people.
And what shall we do?
What *can* we do?

It is all a pity, you must be disappointed,
Go home and do something else for today,
Go home again, go home for today.
For you cannot hear the rabbit, under the earth,
Remarking rather sadly to himself, by himself,
As he rests in his warren, under the earth;
'It won't be long, they are bound to come,
They are bound to come and find me, even here.'

Alan Brownjohn

80 *Wilderness*

There is a wolf in me . . . fangs pointed for tearing gashes . . .
a red tongue for raw meat . . . and the hot lapping of
blood – I keep this wolf because the wilderness gave it to
me and the wilderness will not let it go.

There is a fox in me . . . a silver-gray fox . . . I sniff and
guess . . . I pick things out of the wind and air . . . I nose in
the dark night and take sleepers and eat them and hide the
feathers . . . I circle and loop and double-cross.

There is a hog in me . . . a snout and a belly . . . a machinery
for eating and grunting . . . a machinery for sleeping
satisfied in the sun – I got this too from the wilderness and
the wilderness will not let it go.

There is a fish in me . . . I know I came from salt-blue
water-gates . . . I scurried with shoals of herring . . . I blew
waterspouts with porpoises . . . before land was . . . before
the water went down . . . before Noah . . . before the first
chapter of Genesis.

There is a baboon in me . . . clambering-clawed . . .
   dog-faced . . . yawping a galoot's hunger . . . hairy under
   the armpits . . . here are the hawk-eyed hankering men . . .
   here are the blonde and blue-eyed women . . . here they
   hide curled asleep waiting . . . ready to snarl and kill . . .
   ready to sing and give milk . . . waiting – I keep the
   baboon because the wilderness says so.

There is an eagle in me and a mockingbird . . . and the eagle
   flies among the Rocky Mountains of my dreams and
   fights among the Sierra crags of what I want . . . and the
   mockingbird warbles in the early forenoon before the dew
   is gone, warbles in the underbrush of my Chattanoogas
   of hope, gushes over the blue Ozark foothills of my
   wishes – And I got the eagle and the mockingbird from the
   wilderness.

O, I got a zoo, I got a menagerie, inside my ribs, under my
   bony head, under my red-valve heart – and I got something
   else: it is a man-child heart, a woman-child heart: it is a
   father and mother and lover: it came from God-Knows-
   Where: it is going to God-Knows-Where – For I am the
   keeper of the zoo: I say yes and no: I sing and kill and
   work: I am a pal of the world: I came from the wilderness.

galoot: uncouth fellow

Carl Sandburg

81 *Wires*

The widest prairies have electric fences,
For though old cattle know they must not stray
Young steers are always scenting purer water
Not here but anywhere. Beyond the wires

Leads them to blunder up against the wires
Whose muscle-shredding violence gives no quarter.
Young steers become old cattle from that day,
Electric limits to their widest senses.

Philip Larkin

Acknowledgements

The authors and publisher would like to thank the following for permission to reproduce copyright material:
Dannie Abse: 'Emperors of the Island' from *Tenants of the House* (Century Hutchinson), © Dannie Abse 1957. Reprinted by permission of Anthony Sheil Associates Ltd. Fleur Adcock: 'Nature Table' from *Selected Poems*, © Oxford University Press 1983. Reprinted by permission of Oxford University Press. Earle Birney: 'Answers To A Gradeschool Biology Test' from *Selected Poems 1949–66*. Reprinted by permission of the Canadian Publishers, McClelland & Stuart, Toronto. Ros Barber: 'The Woman in the Breadshop', from *Hardlines 3*. Reprinted by kind permission of Faber and Faber Ltd. James Berry: 'In–A Brixtan–Markit' from *Chain of Days* by James Berry © James Berry 1985. Reprinted by permission of Oxford University Press. David Bowie: 'God Knows I'm Good', © Titanic Music/Chrysalis 1970. Reprinted by permission of Titanic Music/Chrysalis. Pete Brown: 'Few' from *Sprouts on Helicon*, ed. J. Earnshaw (Andre Deutsch 1965). Reprinted by permission of Andre Deutsch Publishers. Alan Brownjohn: 'In This City' and 'We Are Going To See the Rabbit' from *Collected Poems 1958–83*. Reprinted by permission of Century Hutchinson Limited. Jim Burns: 'Message' from *A Simple Flower* (Andium Press). Leonard Cohen: 'A Kite Is a Victim' from *Poems 1956–1968* (Jonathan Cape Ltd). Reprinted by permission of Leonard Cohen. John Cotton: 'The Wilderness' from *Kilroy Was Here* (Chatto & Windus). Reprinted by permission of John Cotton. Jeni Couzyns: 'My Father's Hands' from *Life By Drowning* (Bloodaxe Books 1985). Reprinted by permission of Bloodaxe Books Ltd. Lorner Crozier: 'The Child Who Walks Backwards' from *The Weather* (Coteau Books). Reprinted by permission of McClelland & Stuart, Inc. e.e. cummings: 'there are so many tictoc clocks everywhere...' from *Etcetera*, unpublished poems of e.e. cummings. Reprinted by permission of G. Firmage. Bruce Dawe: 'Search and Destroy' from *Sometimes Gladness, Collected Poems 1954–1987* (Longman Cheshire). 'Mrs Swipe Speaks Out', from *Australian Poety 1980* (Angus & Robertson). Reprinted by permission of Angus & Robertson. Ruth Dallas: 'Photographs of Pioneer Women' (Caxton Press). Reprinted by permission of Ruth Dallas and Caxton Press. Frances Davis: 'Cat'. Reprinted by permission of Frances Davis. Douglas Dunn: 'Landscape With One Figure' from *Terry Street* (Faber 1969). Reprinted by kind permission of Faber and Faber Limited. Clifford Dyment: 'The Snow' from *Poems 1935–48* (J.M. Dent). Reprinted by permission of J.M. Dent Publishers Limited. Gavin Ewart: 'Beginnings' from *The Collected Ewart 1933–1980* (Century Hutchinson). Reprinted by permission of Century Hutchinson Limited. Robert Frost: 'The Road Not Taken' from *The Poetry of Robert Frost*, ed. Edward Connery Latham (Jonathan Cape Ltd). Reprinted by permission of the estate of Robert Frost. Elaine Feinstein: 'Dad' from *Unease & Angels – Selected Poems* (Century Hutchinson). Reprinted by permission of Century Hutchinson Ltd. Mick Gower: 'My Kid Brother' and 'Hero' from *So Far So Good* (William Collins Ltd). Reprinted by permission of James McGibbon. Paul Green: 'for Diz who is 17' from *Sprouts on Helicon*, ed. J. Earnshaw (Andre Deutsch). Reprinted by permission of Andre Deutsch Ltd. Mike Hayhoe: 'City Blues'. Reprinted by permission of Mike Hayhoe. Seamus Heaney: 'Blackberry Picking' from *Death of a Naturalist*. Reprinted by kind permission of Faber and Faber Limited. Richard Hill: 'Cowboy' from *Strictly Private* (Viking Kestrel). Reprinted by permission of Richard Hill. Frances Horovitz: 'Haiku' from *Collected Poems* (Bloodaxe Books 1985). Reprinted by permission of Bloodaxe Books Ltd. A.L. Hendricks: 'Hot Summer Sunday' from *Madonna of the Unknown Nation* (Workshop Press 1974). Reprinted by permission of A.L. Hendricks. Gary Hyland: 'Scrawny's Surefire Acne Cure' from *Just Off Main* (Thistledown Press Ltd). Reprinted by permission of Gary Hyland. Donald Justice: 'Counting the Mad' from *Contemporary American Poetry* (Penguin). Reprinted by permission of Donald Justice and Wesleyan University Press. Jenny Joseph: 'Kite' from Rose in the Afternoon (J.M. Dent & Sons). Reprinted by permission of John Johnson (Authors' Agent) Limited. Richard Kell: 'Pigeons' from *Differences* (Chatto & Windus Ltd); 'Fishing Harbour Towards Evening' from *Control Tower* (Chatto & Windus Ltd). Reprinted by permission of Richard Kell. Bernard Kops: 'And Peace Will Come', 'Moment' from *For the Record* (Secker & Warburg). Reprinted by permission of Martin, Secker & Warburg. John Kitching: 'City' from *Standpoints* (Nelson Harrap). Reprinted by permission of John Kitching. Philip Larkin: 'Wires' from *The Less Deceived* (Marvell Press). Reprinted by permission of The Marvell Press.

Sue Lenier: 'Birds' from *Swan Song* (Oleander Press). Reprinted by kind permission of Oleander Press and Sue Lenier. Don Linehan: 'The Lesson' from *Birds of Fire* (Owl's Head Press). Reprinted by permission of Don Linehan and Owl's Head Press. Liz Loxley: 'The Thickness of Ice' from *Hardlines 2* (Faber and Faber). Reprinted by kind permission of Faber and Faber Limited. Norman MacCaig: 'Sounds of the Day' and 'Movements' from *Collected Poems* (Chatto & Windus Ltd). Reprinted by permission of Norman MacCaig. Walter De La Mare: John Mouldy. Reprinted by permission of The Literary Trustees of Walter De La Mare and the Society of Authors as their representative. Roger McGough: 'Nooligan' and 'First Day At School' from *In The Glass Room* (Jonathan Cape). 'Cowboy' from *Strictly Private* (Penguin); 'Bye Bye Blacksheep' from *Melting Into the Foreground* (Penguin). Reprinted by permission of the Peters, Frasers & Dunlop Group Limited. Adrian Mitchell: 'Fifteen Million Plastic Bags', 'A Curse on My Former Bank Manager' and 'Dumb Insolence'. Reprinted by permission of Adrian Mitchell and Allison & Busby. Mary di Michele: 'As In the Beginning' from *Necessary Sugar* (Oberon Press). Reprinted by permission of Oberon Press. Rosalie Moore: 'Catalogue' from *New Yorker Magazine*. Reprinted by permission; © 1940, 1968 The New Yorker Magazine, Inc. Edwin Morgan: 'Strawberries' from *Scottish Poetry No. 1* (Carcanet Press). Reprinted by permission of Edwin Morgan. Oswald Mashali: 'Pigeons at the Oppenheimer Park' and 'The Face of Hunger' from *Sound of a Cowhide Drum* (Renoster Press). Reprinted by permission of Renoster Press. Alden Nowlan 'The Mysterious Naked Man' and 'Police Beat' from *The Mysterious Naked Man*; 'Looking for Nancy' from *Under the Ice*; 'The Execution' from *The Things Which Are* (Clark, Irwin & Co.) Reprinted by permission of Clark, Irwin & Co. Grace Nichols: 'Be A Butterfly' from *The Fat Black Women's Poems* (Virago). Reprinted by permission Virago Press and Grace Nichols. Philip Oakes: 'Spiders' from *Married/Singular* (Andre Deutsch). Vasco Popa: 'Proverbs' from *The Golden Apple* (Anvil Press Poetry 1980). William Plomer: 'Move On' from *Collected Poems* (Jonathan Cape). Reprinted by permission of the estate of William Plomer. Andy Pearmain: 'Mr and Mrs' from *Hardlines 3* (Faber). Reprinted by kind permission of Faber and Faber Limited. Dorothy Parker: 'One Perfect Rose' from *The Portable Dorothy Parker* (Duckworth). Reprinted by permission of Gerald Duckworth & Co. Limited. Mark Roberts: 'Videodrone' from *Hardlines 3* (Faber). Reprinted by permission of Faber and Faber Limited. Magaly Sanchez:' Almost Love' from *Breaking the Silences*, 20th Century Cuban Poetry, trs by M. Randall (Pulp Press). Vernon Scannell: 'Mastering the Craft' from *Winterlude* (Robson Books); 'Incendiary' from *Epithets of War* (Eyre & Spottiswood). Reprinted by permission of Robson Books Ltd. Louis Simpson: 'The Battle' from *Good News of Death* from N.Y. Scribners 1955. Stevie Smith: 'The Jungle Husband', 'The Wanderer', 'Anger's Freeing Power' from *The Collected Poems of Stevie Smith* (Penguin Modern Classics). Reprinted by permission of James MacGibbon (the executor). Marin Sorescu: 'It's Going to Rain' from *Selected Poems by Marin Sorescu*, trs by Michael Hamburger (Bloodaxe Books 1983). Reprinted by permission of Bloodaxe Books Ltd. William Stafford: 'Fifteen' from *The Rescued Year* (Harper & Row). Reprinted by permission of Harper & Row Publishers Ltd. May Swenson: 'The Secret In The Cat'. Reprinted by permission of I.R.R. Knudson for the Estate of May Swenson. Ts'ao Sung: 'Written In the Year Chi-hai (879)' from *The Penguin Book of Chinese Verse* trs by Robert Kotewall and Norman L. Smith (Penguin Books 1962) © N.L. Smith and R.H. Kotewall 1962. Chen Tzu-Lung: 'The Little Cart' from *170 Chinese Poems* by Arthur Waley (Constable Publishers). A.S.J. Tessimond: 'Cats' and 'Daydream' from *Voices In A Giant City* (William Heinemann). R.S. Thomas: 'Soil'. Reprinted by permission of Gwydian Thomas. Sojourner Truth: 'Ain't I A Woman?' from *Black Sister – Poetry by Black American Women 1746–1980* (Indiana University Press). Kath Walker: 'We Are Going' from *My People* (Jacaranda Wiley Ltd). Andrew Young: 'Hard Frost' from *Collected Poems* (Secker & Warburg). Yevgeni Yevtushenko: 'Waiting' from *Selected Poems* trs by Robin Milner-Gulland and Peter Levi (Penguin Books 1962) © Robin Milner-Gulland and Peter Levi, 1962).

It has not been possible to trace all copyright holders. The authors and publisher would be glad to hear from any unacknowledged sources at the first opportunity.